THE
ULTIMATE
CHRISTMAS ACTIVITY BOOK

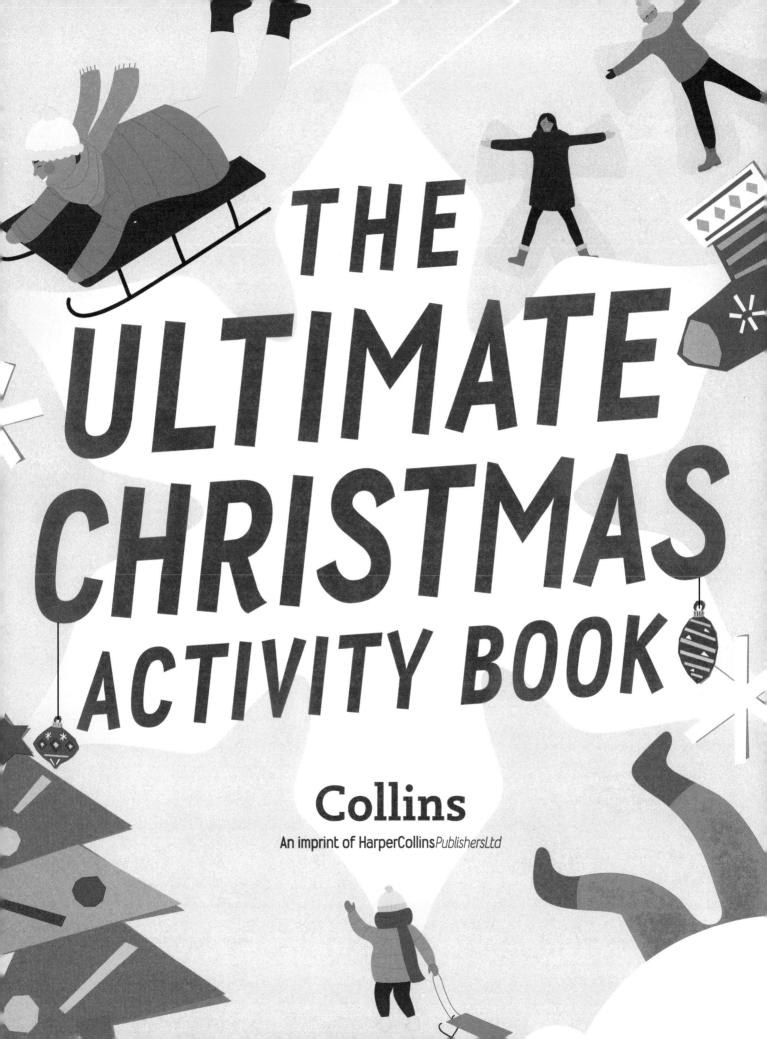

THE ULTIMATE CHRISTMAS ACTIVITY BOOK

Collins

An imprint of HarperCollinsPublishersLtd

The Ultimate Christmas Activity Book
Copyright © 2024 by HarperCollins Publishers Ltd.
All rights reserved.

Published by Collins, an imprint of HarperCollins Publishers Ltd

First edition

Illustrations (mazes, seek-and-find, and how-to-draw features) by Paul Covello
Holiday Crafts material copyright © 2024 by Marthe Jocelyn
Text by Hadley Dyer, Zanne Klingenberg, Dan Liebman, and Duncan McKenzie

All artwork Shutterstock except pages 8—9, 18—19, 22—23, 24—25, 28—29, 33, 39,
40—41, 48—49, 52—53, 54—55, 61, 62—63, 64—65, 68—69, 75, 78—79, 84—85,
88—89, 92—93, 98—99, 101, 103—105, 107, 109, 110—115, 120—128

HarperCollins books may be purchased for educational, business, or sales promotional
use through our Special Markets Department.

HarperCollins Publishers Ltd
Bay Adelaide Centre, East Tower
22 Adelaide Street West, 41st Floor
Toronto, Ontario, Canada
M5H 4E3

www.harpercollins.ca

ISBN 978-1-4434-7230-2

Printed and bound in Canada

TC 9 8 7 6 5 4 3 2 1

GETTING STARTED

This book belongs to

_____

Welcome to this festive activity book
packed with holiday fun!

To use this book, you'll need:
a pencil or pen
coloured pencils or crayons
a little imagination

READY TO JINGLE? LET'S GET STARTED!

SANTA'S WORKSHOP

There are holiday words *ho-ho*-hidden in the letters below. See if you can find the words from the list all by your-*elf*!

BELLS
CHRISTMAS
ELVES

GIVING
HELPERS
JOLLY

LIST
NAUGHTY
NICE

NORTH POLE
PRESENT

C B A G A O H O O A C S W J C
D Z V T G M C V W N L T B D J
L M H Q H Q V W N A U G H T Y
T L N I X A M B L X G U U I Y
J N J O E H Y S M T G C H Y Z
W M O P R E S E N T I H L W H
L C Z R I N O J S N V R X I C
X Q Y P T H P U P N I I Y D F
F M G J K H E U Q I N S Y B D
G J O L L Y P L X C G T X V Z
X O Y Q I W B O P E G M S D Y
H E Y X L Q C E L E A A R Z L
I K Y K X R C I L E R S B B I
C G M C W W L C H L S S A B S
V T O Z E L V E S I S Q W M T

Stuck? See solution on page 120

NORTH POLE ANIMALS

Can you find the names of the animals from the list in the letters below?
Some of them are *polar*-ly, *bear*-ly hidden!

CARIBOU	MOOSE	ORCA	TERN
LEMMING	MUSKOX	PUFFIN	WALRUS
LYNX	NARWHAL	SEAL	WOLF

```
P  O  H  C  B  P  B  V  L  Y  N  X  L  R  E
N  H  Y  A  K  Z  R  H  Z  L  R  O  O  P  M
A  W  V  R  K  B  C  P  X  E  E  W  M  A  U
R  U  P  I  A  A  D  O  Q  M  Q  O  O  F  S
W  A  B  B  N  O  P  R  B  M  M  L  O  T  K
H  B  V  O  W  S  E  C  P  I  T  F  S  S  O
A  M  I  U  A  P  A  A  J  N  E  J  E  X  X
L  Q  C  G  L  U  L  X  Q  G  Q  M  E  Q  G
T  G  U  N  R  F  W  V  G  D  W  M  G  U  B
Q  T  R  X  U  F  F  Z  Y  K  H  E  M  W  E
N  Q  N  T  S  I  Z  J  X  W  T  R  E  T  K
N  F  P  D  S  N  Q  J  F  N  K  B  F  D  Y
M  H  C  L  Q  H  Z  Q  D  C  K  Q  O  P  P
X  F  Q  S  E  A  L  L  N  O  W  B  L  U  M
Z  O  C  F  X  L  T  Z  T  E  R  N  L  Q  J
```

Stuck? See solution on page 120

THE NORTH POLE

There is *snow* way that you can find all the items hidden in this icy illustration. What do your elf eyes see? **CLUES: 6 SNOWMEN • 10 ICE CREAM CONES • 7 ELVES • 10 MICE • 4 SCARVES • 5 SEALS**

Stuck? See solution on page 120

Barbie

Kids around the world love playing with dolls, and no doll is more famous than Barbie. Barbie is named after the daughter of her creator, and Barbie's full name is Barbara Millicent Roberts. She's more than just a doll, though. She's an inspiration. Before Barbie, the only dolls that kids played with were babies. Barbie was the first grown-up doll that kids could play with and imagine who they could be when they grew up. Barbie's creator first got the idea when she saw her daughter playing with paper dolls and dressing them up in different clothes. She thought, "Why isn't there a real doll like that?" Then she got to work. Barbie's creator was the co-founder of the toy company Mattel and was also the company's first president.

Barbie has always stirred up trouble. Some people love Barbie because she did things that no dolls had done before, like show that girls are independent and can have cool jobs. But other people worry that she hasn't done enough to change things. Maybe she has too many clothes, cars, and houses, which isn't good for the planet, or maybe she doesn't show enough different types of bodies or colours of skin. It is important for kids to be able to find dolls that look like them so that they can

imagine what kind of person they want to be. But Barbie has been around for over 60 years, and she has changed a lot in that time. Mattel has introduced many versions of Barbie, as well as many friends of hers, that represent more people and even introduced dolls that look like important women from history, such as Amelia Earhart, Frida Kahlo, and Jane Goodall.

DID YOU KNOW?

Barbie has had over 250 jobs, including doctor, astronaut, pilot, athlete, and executive, and she has even run for president of the United States!

TRIVIA

✓X✓X✓X✓X✓X✓X✓X✓X

1. What is the name of Barbie's creator?
(A) Barbara Handler
(B) Christina Handler
(C) Ruth Handler

2. Who was Ken named after?
(A) The creator's son
(B) A family friend
(C) The family dog

3. Barbie's inspiration (the Lilli doll) and her biggest collector both come from what country?
(A) England
(B) Germany
(C) Canada

Answers: 1. (C) Ruth Handler; 2. (A) The creator's son; 3. (B) Germany

Let's Play Merry Mash-up!

Pine-ing to tell a holiday story? Look no *fir*-ther than this fill-in-the-blanks game!

Before you read the story, fill out the requested list of words. Remember to use the type of word called for. *Yule* then add these words to the blank spaces in the story.

You could also ask a friend to gift you the list of words. Don't let them see the story first! Then, write the words in the blank spaces of the story—and *tree*-t your-*elves* to a laugh!

The Words You'll Need

Your last name:_____

Adjective:_____

Family member's name:_____

Place:_____

Verb past tense:_____

Family member's name:_____

Verb ending in -ing:_____

Family member's name:_____

Verb ending in -ing:_____

Plural noun:_____

Feeling:_____

What's That Word?

Here are the types of words you might need to complete each story.

A **noun** describes a person, place, or thing. For example: grandmother, workshop, or cookie.

When we ask for a **plural noun**, that means more than one of that person, place, or thing. For example: grandmothers, workshops, or cookies.

An **adjective** describes a noun. For example: small, silly, or yummy.

A **verb** describes an action. For example: sing, giggle, or dance. We might ask for a **verb** in the **past tense**, such as sang, giggled, or danced. Or the verb could end in -ing, such as singing, giggling, or dancing.

An **adverb** describes how an action is done. It often ends in -ly. For example: slowly, quickly, or suddenly. Some examples of adverbs that don't end in -ly are sometimes, before, and very.

Sometimes we'll be more specific about the type of word you need. For example, we might ask for a type of animal or food.

CHRISTMAS NEWSLETTER

Welcome to the _____'s (your last name) **annual Christmas**

newsletter! We're delighted to share all the_____ (adjective)

things we did this past year. _____ (family member's name) **went**

to a(n) _____ (place) **and** _____ (verb past tense)

like a champ. _____ (family member's name) **won a**

_____ (verb ending in -ing) **competition! And** _____

(family member's name) **passed a(n)** _____ (verb ending in -ing)

test with flying _____ (plural noun).

Not to brag, but our family makes us so _____ (feeling).

HOLIDAY MOVIES

Complete the *mistletoe*-tally festive movie titles to solve the crossword puzzle.

ACROSS:

3. *A* _____ *Called Christmas.*
4. Brother and sister try to catch Santa in *The Christmas* _____ .
5. Skeleton discovers what Christmas is like in *The* _____ *Before Christmas.*
10. Santa's last name spelled with a "K."
11. Santa's clumsy son goes on an adventure with Grandsanta in _____ *Christmas.*
12. About a train call *The Polar* _____ .

DOWN:

1. About an alien named Oh, only at Christmas, _____ *For the Holidays.*
2. _____ *The Snowman* comes to life through a magic hat.
6. Green furry meanie, *Dr. Seuss's The* _____.
7. Angel with some extra letters: her Christmas.
8. Story about Buddy, who is too big to be an _____.
9. Elves get homes ready for Santa's arrival in _____ *& Landing.*

Stuck? See solution on page 120

Stuck? See solution on page 121

ACROSS:

2. Let It _____.
4. Rudolph the Red-Nosed _____ .
7. Walking in a Winter _____.
9. I _____ a Hippopotamus for Christmas.
12. _____ the Halls.

DOWN:

1. The _____ Days of Christmas.
3. _____ Bells.
5. Santa Claus Is Coming to _____.
6. Feliz _____.
8. Jingle Bell _____.
10. _____ in a Manger.
11. All I Want for Christmas Is My Two Front _____.

Fill in the blanks of these song titles to complete the *holly*-day crossword.

CHRISTMAS SONGS

WINTER SPORTS

Find the wintry words hidden in the letters below. Keep looking until you *snow* where they all are!

HOCKEY
ICE FISHING
LUGE

SKATE
SKI
SLEDDING

SNOWBOARD
SNOWMOBILE
SNOWSHOE

TOBOGGAN

H N A K Z S N O W M O B I L E
S L U G E I L X S W C U Y S L
N U F S Z W C V O H Q E X K G
O T B I N D H E E H I V S A P
W F C W R O R O F D J C L T L
S K O Y A J W G C I G M E E E
H T Y T H T L B Z K S E D D S
O L O S U P S H O P E H D T K
E S R B X B G J N A K Y I D I
H U B J O U E D Y S R B N N X
K Q E E F G N D N J Y D G S G
M C Y U D C G A J S X B B W C
X I X Q H I F A D O O I S F R
Y B M D K B A M N T B S P T C
W C U E D A J W C X J C L G L

Stuck? See solution on page 121

WHAT IS YOUR ELF NAME?

Have you ever wondered what your name would be if you were a holly jolly little helper in Santa's workshop?

Find out below by finding the first letter of your first name and combining that elf name with the name that goes with your favourite colour. Have two favourite colours? See what happens when you combine two last names!

A Anise
B Bellsby
C Cakey
D Dolly
E Eggnog
F Freckle
G Ginger
H Hurdy-Gurdy
I Icicle
J Jeronimo
K Kupkate
L Lolly
M Minty

N Nougat
U Ube
P Prinkle
Q Quexin
R Ribbin
S Sparkles
T Tinker
U Umbrelly
V Vanilla
W Wiffles
X Xoxo
Y Yolo
Z Zazz

RED Ruffles
ORANGE Elfton
YELLOW Fitzpresent
WHITE Decemberberg
BLUE Nicholastein
PURPLE Mistletoast
RAINBOW McFruitcake
GREY Kringleski
GREEN El Noël
BLACK Van Der Pine
BROWN Nutcracker
PINK Twinkleoff
GOLD Von Frostbite
SILVER Snovich

HOW TO DRAW A CHRISTMAS TREE

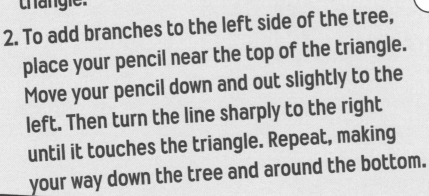

1. A great Christmas tree starts by drawing a tall triangle.

2. To add branches to the left side of the tree, place your pencil near the top of the triangle. Move your pencil down and out slightly to the left. Then turn the line sharply to the right until it touches the triangle. Repeat, making your way down the tree and around the bottom.

3. Repeat step #2 on the right side of the triangle.

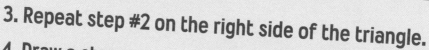

4. Draw a star, an angel, or another ornament at the top of the triangle. Add two short vertical lines at the bottom of the triangle to make a tree trunk.

5. Add a short, slightly curved line to the bottom of the tree trunk. Then create a tree skirt around the base of the tree. The tree skirt can be any shape, including a wide triangle with a wavy bottom side.

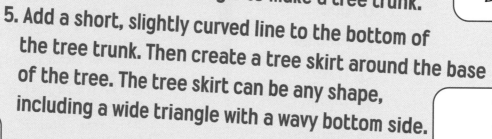

6. Draw wavy lines across the front of the tree. Add small dots to the strings to create lights. The light shapes can be ovals or circles. You could add other ornaments too—it's up to you!

7. Colour in your tree and prepare to be dazzled!

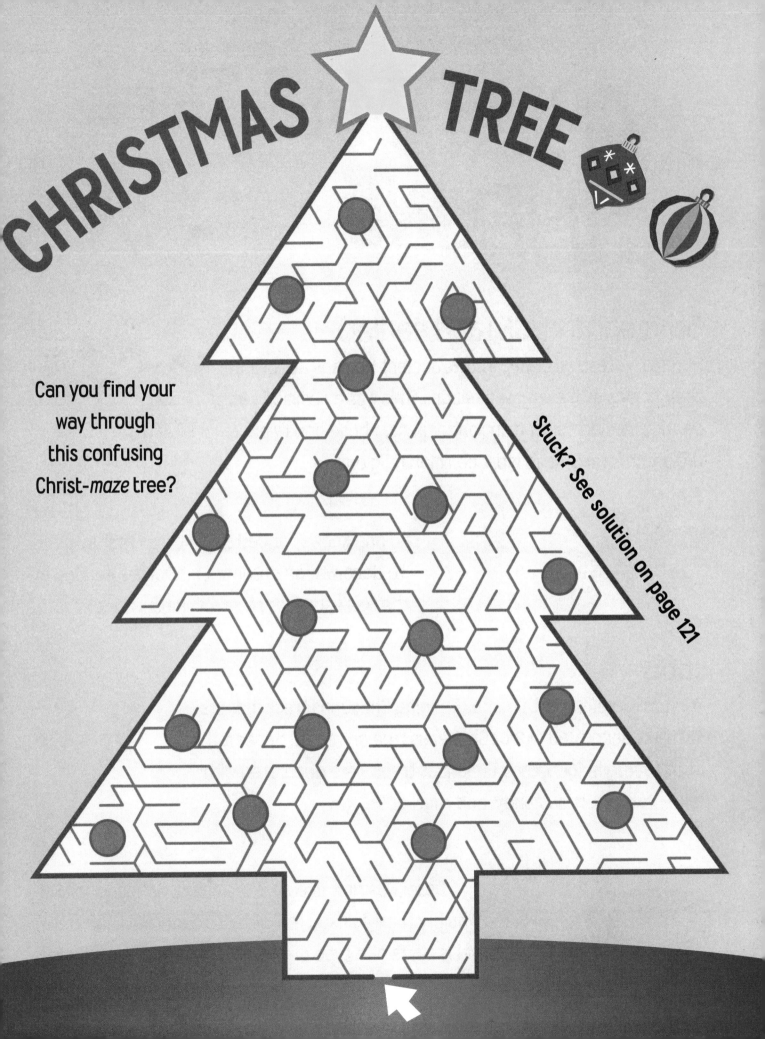

CHRISTMAS ★ TREE

Can you find your way through this confusing Christ-*maze* tree?

Stuck? See solution on page 121

A CHRISTMAS TREE TIMELINE

5th century BCE (and earlier)

During the festival of Saturnalia, ancient Romans decorated their homes with evergreen boughs. This was a common winter solstice tradition among ancient pagans, whose gods were different from today's most common religions.

1510

No one knows for certain who was first inspired to decorate an outdoor Christmas tree. One of the earliest records is from Riga, Latvia, in 1510.

1605

We have Germany to thank for bringing Christmas trees indoors. The first decorated indoor Christmas tree on record appeared in Strasburg in 1605. Early Christmas trees were decorated with paper flowers, fruit, candy, and small gifts.

1610

Tinsel was first used in Nuremburg, Germany, in 1610. Wealthy families used real silver to decorate their trees! Today, tinsel is made of a type of plastic called polyvinyl chloride.

1781

Sorel, Québec, was the site of the first North American Christmas tree in 1781. The tradition was brought to Québec from Germany by Baron Frederich Riedesel and his wife, Baroness Frederika. They put up the tree for a Christmas Eve party they held for German and British military officers.

1848

Queen Victoria of England and her German husband, Prince Albert, made Christmas trees popular in England. In 1848, a picture was published of the royal family with their tree, sparking a trend that has never faded. From England, Christmas trees spread to other countries, including Canada. Mass produced tree ornaments began appearing just a few years later.

1880

You might know that Thomas Edison invented the lightbulb, but did you know he also helped invent Christmas lights? In 1880, Edison placed a strand of lights outside his laboratory during the Christmas season. In 1882, his business partner, Edward H. Johnson, created electric string lights for trees.

1917

On December 6, 1917, an explosion rocked Halifax Harbour after two ships collided. Thousands of people were injured and killed. The city of Boston acted fast, sending medical teams and supplies. Every year since, Nova Scotia has sent a giant Christmas tree to Boston in thanks.

gingerbread house

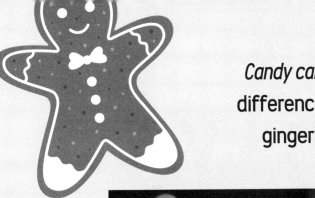

Candy cane you find all six differences between these gingerbread houses?

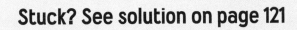

Stuck? See solution on page 121

HOLIDAY CRAFTS

SNOW DAYS

Nature is the sneakiest artist of all, especially when it comes to snow. Inspiration is everywhere! As long as you bundle up, playing outside can be one of the best parts of the holidays.

What You Need
Warm clothes
Imagination
Snow!

What to Do
Turn damp, heavy snow—sometimes called packing snow—into balls and other shapes. This is the best kind of snow for making snowpeople, and it sticks well to trees and poles.

Fresh snow is a blank canvas. Use your feet to stamp shapes and designs in your yard or a local park.

A stick or hand is all you need to draw faces on snow-covered tree trunks, park benches, or stoops. You can also make faces out of leaves, twigs, and other small objects. Tree needles make great hair!

Tip: You may want to add some extra snow to a surface before making a face!

WORD SCRAMBLE

Holly smokes! The letters in these holiday words are scrambled! Can you put them back in the correct order? Some letters are already in place to help get you started. Turn the page upside down to see the completed words.

GONGEG	E_ _N_G
BROBIN	_IB_O_
KURTYE	T_ R _ E_
GENERDARBIG	_I_G_ _B_ _AD
FEL	_ _F
TENNAROM	_R_A_EN_
RATHEW	WR_ _ _ _ _
TOMESTILE	M_ _TLE_ _ _ _
KINGTOCS	_ _O_K_ _G
ERET	_ R _ E

THE NUTCRACKER

Can you crack the case of the nutty words hidden in the letters below?

ANGEL   FAIRY   MICE   PRINCE
BALLET   FLOWER   NUTCRACKER   SOLDIER
CLARA   KING   OWL   SUGARPLUM

```
D  N  L  N  U  T  C  R  A  C  K  E  R  H  J
T  V  S  P  R  I  N  C  E  E  Z  T  D  Y  J
I  O  U  I  G  W  K  T  A  L  W  W  H  I  A
V  D  G  P  D  B  A  L  L  E  T  K  H  D  U
G  F  A  H  S  E  J  V  Y  K  D  W  F  D  A
Z  G  R  B  V  R  O  S  S  I  T  H  Y  Y  F
Y  X  P  B  S  O  L  D  I  E  R  H  Q  G  A
O  W  L  D  I  V  B  H  O  A  P  X  Q  Y  I
M  I  U  A  N  G  E  L  W  Q  K  Y  F  K  R
C  I  M  O  Q  Q  C  R  L  O  C  I  W  P  Y
H  N  C  G  Q  M  I  R  B  U  L  K  N  R  D
U  F  T  E  K  V  Y  K  A  D  A  R  L  G  W
G  R  W  R  P  I  Y  R  B  N  R  S  Y  K  X
W  O  Y  P  G  Y  M  L  H  Q  A  M  I  N  T
L  D  W  V  F  L  O  W  E  R  X  N  A  F  H
```

Stuck? See solution on page 121

SNOW DIFFERENCE

Can you find 15 changes in these two snow scenes?

Stuck? See solution on page 122

Play-Doh

Whether you roll out a snake or sculpt a dinosaur, Play-Doh is fun to squish and shape. And kids have been doing that for a long time: Play-Doh has been sold as a kids' toy for over 60 years. Before it was made for kids, though, it was made for cleaning! Back in the early 1900s, keeping your house warm meant burning wood or coal. Soot from burning coal got all over everything. The company Kutol sold soft, squishy stuff that could be used to wipe soot off wallpaper. They became the largest wallpaper cleaner company in the world for a while. In the 1950s, people found cleaner ways to heat their houses, and wallpaper started to be made from easier-to-clean materials like vinyl. Kutol was in trouble because no one wanted to buy their product. Fortunately, the sister-in-law of one of the company's leaders was a teacher. She knew that the wallpaper cleaner was also fun for her students to play with. Now Play-Doh makes messes instead of cleaning them!

Play-Doh today hasn't changed much from the kind played with in 1956. There is less salt in it now so that it doesn't dry out quickly. That's the only change in the recipe. Play-Doh comes in at least 65 colours,

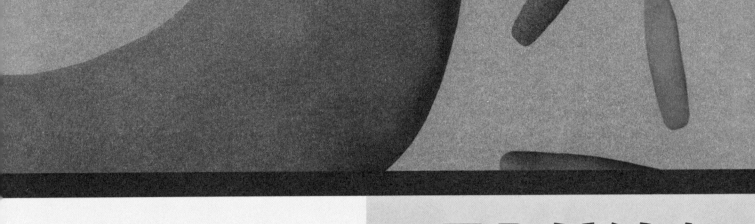

and it has sold more as a modelling dough than it ever did as a wallpaper cleaner. Over 3 billion cans of Play-Doh have been made. If you stacked those cans, they could reach the moon six times! According to some people, if you took the dough out of those cans and squished it through the Play-Doh Fun Factory, it would make a snake that could wrap around the earth 300 times!

DID YOU KNOW?
The smell of Play-Doh was made into a perfume for the 50th anniversary of Play-Doh.

TRIVIA
✓X✓X✓X✓X✓X✓X✓X✓X

1. If you made a gigantic ball out of all the Play-Doh that has ever been made, how much would it weigh?
(A) 1 million pounds
(B) 700 million pounds
(C) 1 billion pounds

2. How do you get rid Play-Doh stuck in the carpet?
(A) You can't. It's a new decoration for your house
(B) Lasers
(C) Let it dry then use a stiff brush to loosen it

3. How many colours of Play-Doh were there originally?
(A) 1
(B) 6
(C) 10

Answers: 1. (B); 2. (C) ; 3. (A) 1—White

HOLIDAY DINNER

Can you guess what delectable dishes these curious clues are conjuring to complete the crossword?

ACROSS:

3. Often mashed.
4. Historically known as "milk punch," a popular holiday drink.
7. Pumpkin and apple are popular.
8. Made with breadcrumbs, inside the turkey.
10. Has fruit in it at Christmas.
12. The red sauce eaten with turkey.

DOWN:

1. Can be chocolate chip or shortbread.
2. Salty or smoked meat.
5. Long and skinny type of bean, named after its colour.
6. Roasted bird.
9. Pour it from a boat.
11. Orange potato.

Stuck? See solution on page 122

HOW TO DRAW AN ELF

1. Start by drawing a circle for a face and attaching a bell-shaped body. Add a pair of curved elf ears to each side of the face. Draw a pair of horizonal lines on each side of the body for arms. A pair of vertical lines on the bottom of the body will become the legs.

2. Now, add details to the elf's clothes. These include a pair of cuffs at the ends of the arms, shoes at the bottom of the legs, and a little collar under the elf's chin. Don't worry if your elf shoes aren't fancy. Any shoes will do!

3. What will your elf's face look like? Will the eyes be big or small? Will the nose be long or short? Will the mouth be smiling or frowning? Add a few tufts of hair to the elf's head. Two lines that run across the body will form the top and bottom of a belt. Another line, running just above the bottom of the body, will create a hemline.

4. Place a little square in the middle of the belt to create a buckle. Add mitts on the ends of the cuffs, and the base of a hat to the elf's head.

5. The rest of the hat can be pointy, swirly, or any shape you like! Add a square to one of the elf's mittens.

6. Nearly done! Draw a bow or ribbon on the box to transform it into a present. Add a tiny jingle bell to the top of the hat and a candy cane to the elf's free hand.

7. Finish by adding colours and pattern to the drawing to bring the elf to life!

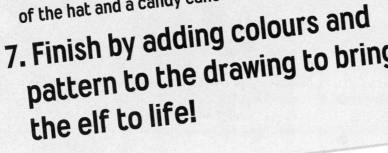

MERRY MASH-UP

How to Play
Before you read the story, fill out the requested list of words. Then, use these words to fill the blank spaces in the story. Want to supercharge the fun? Play with a friend! Ask them to give you each type of word on the list. Write their answers in the blank spaces of the story—and laugh until your belly shakes like a bowlful of jelly!

The Words You'll Need
Person in the room:_____

Plural noun:_____

Alphabet letter:_____

Adverb:_____

Verb:_____

Verb ending in -ing:_____

Plural noun:_____

Verb ending in -ing:_____

Verb ending in -ing:_____

Adjective:_____

Noun:_____

ELF REPORT CARD

Supervisor: Mrs. Claus

Name: Elf _____ (person in the room) **Sparkle Pants**

Department: _____ (plural noun)

Grade: _____ **+** (alphabet letter)

Comments: _____ (same person in the room) **Sparkle Pants**

works very _____ (adverb)**. So quick to** _____ (verb)**!**

So good at _____ (verb ending in -ing)**!**

_____ (same person in the room) **could talk less about**

_____ (plural noun) **around the workshop. And practise**

_____ (verb ending in -ing) **and** _____ (verb ending in -ing)**.**

But overall, Elf _____ (same person in the room)

Sparkle Pants is a(n) _____ (adjective) **toy maker.**

That _____ (noun) **truly sparkles!**

TREE DECORATIONS

Search for the *tree*-cky words hidden in the letters below. Can you find them all?

BELLS   ICICLE   PINE CONE   STAR
CANDY CANE   LIGHTS   POINSETTIA   TINSEL
GARLAND   ORNAMENT   SLEIGH

```
E  V  R  P  I  N  E  C  O  N  E  K  Z  S  A
U  Z  T  G  Y  Y  T  J  C  O  S  I  L  Z  S
C  I  R  Y  Z  N  L  D  A  O  Y  N  Z  F  X
C  C  R  V  M  S  R  B  N  H  P  E  M  S  M
T  P  V  Z  K  A  Z  O  D  C  O  X  Q  T  U
O  R  N  A  M  E  N  T  Y  X  I  B  U  A  P
G  U  W  R  Y  V  B  A  C  W  N  E  A  R  L
K  T  V  I  O  B  Q  Q  A  A  S  L  S  Z  T
G  M  Q  F  C  G  W  Z  N  C  E  L  L  M  H
T  A  G  A  M  I  K  S  E  J  T  S  M  L  T
I  S  R  Z  V  T  C  H  P  W  T  V  L  I  S
N  D  V  L  B  T  J  L  R  Y  I  B  B  G  V
S  X  T  K  A  C  T  L  E  K  A  Y  R  H  W
E  S  V  Y  S  N  Q  S  L  E  I  G  H  T  I
L  G  B  N  L  S  D  V  K  E  K  R  Z  S  H
```

Stuck? See solution on page 122

WANTED

Age: Unknown
Hair: Unknown (covered by hat), white beard
Eyes: Twinkly
Build: Short, with a jiggly belly
Clothes: Fur covered in ashes and soot

SANTA CLAUS

FOR: Driving a sleigh above the speed limit, parking illegally on rooftops, breaking and entering, spreading joy without a permit

ARMED WITH: A small pipe and sack of unknown contents

RUNS WITH: Mrs. Claus, a gang of nine reindeer, and many elves

LAST SEEN: Heading in the direction of the North Pole

WARNING! If you see this person, you are up past your bedtime on Christmas Eve. Go to sleep straight away to avoid being added to the naughty list.

ALSO GOES BY

Papai Noel	Brazil
Dun Che Lao Ren	China
Saint Nicholas	Multiple countries
Père Noël	France, Quebec
Der Weihnachtsmann	Germany
Babbo Natale	Italy
Sinterklaas	The Netherlands
Pai Natal	Portugal
Father Christmas	United Kingdom
Kris Kringle	United States
Noel Baba	Turkey

CHRISTMAS TRIVIA

Ready to put your Christmas *noël*-edge to the test? Choose the answer to each question from one of the three options provided. Turn this the page upside down to check how many you got right.

1. Where were Christmas crackers invented?
(A) United States
(B) England
(C) Brazil

2. What's the most popular main dish for Christmas dinner in North America?
(A) Ham
(B) Goose
(C) Turkey

3. How many days are on most advent calendars?
(A) 12—one for each of the twelve days of Christmas
(B) 24 or 25—one for each day of December up to Christmas Eve or Christmas Day
(C) 31—one for every day of December

4. What type of drink is eggnog?
(A) Milk punch
(B) Egg smoothie
(C) Cream shake

5. What is the most popular Christmas meal in Japan?
(A) Sushi
(B) Roast beef
(C) KFC

6. Traditionally, what's supposed to happen when two people stand together under a sprig of mistletoe?
(A) They bow or curtsy
(B) They kiss
(C) They promise to exchange small gifts

Answers: 1. (B) England; 2. (C) Turkey; 3. (B) 24 or 25; 4. (A) Milk punch; 5. (C) KFC; 6. (B) They kiss

Find your way through this frosty maze for a jolly, happy time.

SNOWMAN

Stuck? See solution on page 122

HOLIDAY CRAFTS

TINFOIL LEAVES, BIRDS, FISH, AND MORE!

Traditional Mexican tin ornaments are a type of folk art made of thin pieces of tin. You can make your own version using ordinary tinfoil.

What You Need

3 pieces of medium-weight (or 2 pieces of heavy-weight) tinfoil, cut into equal-sized squares

Glue stick

Scissors

Dull pencil with a rounded tip

Paper punch or scissors

Hangers: Pieces of string, ribbon, or dental floss, or partially unbent paper clips

Cutting Shapes

You can cut your tinfoil into any shape you like! It helps to draw the shape with a pencil first, pressing just hard enough to slightly dent the tinfoil. You can then follow the outline of the shape with your scissors.

What to Do

1. Place a piece of tinfoil on a flat surface with its shiny side down, dull side up.
2. Apply the glue stick in even strokes to the entire surface of the dull side.
3. Place another sheet of foil on top of the first one, lining up their edges. This time, place the dull side down, shiny side up.
4. If using heavy-weight tinfoil, skip to step #5. If using medium-weight tinfoil, repeat steps #2 and #3 with a third piece of tinfoil.
5. Allow the glue to set.
6. Cut shapes out of the stacked tinfoil. (See "Cutting Shapes.")
7. Emboss each shape with designs by gently pressing the rounded tip of a dull pencil into the foil. (See tips below.)
8. Use the paper punch or scissors to pierce a hole close to one edge of the ornament.
9. Run a hanger through the hole.
10. Tie or twist the ends of your hanger together.

Using a Template

This book includes two pages of templates that can be used to create fun shapes for your tinfoil ornaments (see page 128). To use a template:

1. Lay a thin sheet of paper over a template.
2. Trace the shape onto the paper with a pencil.
3. Cut the shape out of the paper.
3. Place the paper shape over a piece of tinfoil.
4. Trace around the edges of the paper shape with a pencil so that the tinfoil is slightly dented.
5. Cut the shape out of the tinfoil, following the dented outline.

MERRY MASH-UP

How to Play

Before you read the story, fill out the requested list of words. Then, use these words to fill the blank spaces in the story. Want to supercharge the fun? Play with a friend! Ask them to give you each type of word on the list. Write their answers in the blank spaces of the story—and laugh until your belly shakes like a bowlful of jelly!

The Words You'll Need

Adjective:_____

Adjective:_____

Adjective:_____

Room in the home:_____

Person in room:_____

Number:_____

Noun:_____

Noun:_____

Person in room:_____

Body part:_____

TRIMMING THE TREE

The holiday season is so _____ (adjective) **with a**

Christmas tree. The best trees are _____ (adjective)

but not too _____ (adjective) **. I like to set up the tree**

in the _____ (room in home), **so it has plenty of space.**

Last year, _____ (person in room) **put on**

_____ (number) **ornaments, so I'd better keep**

a(n) _____ (noun) **on them. When it's time to put the**

_____ (noun) **on top, I'll climb on** _____ (person in room)**'s**

_____ (body part), **and we'll hang it together with love.**

FESTIVE FUNNIES

What do you call a disrespectful
reindeer? *RUDE—OLPH*

Where do Santa and the elves go
for a swim? *THE NORTH POOL*

FACE THE MUSIC

Are you a Christmas music master? Or happy to just hum along? Fill in the missing words from these popular Christmas songs to test how well you know them. Turn the page upside down to check how many you got right.

"White Christmas"

I'm _____ of a white Christmas
Just like the ones I used to know
Where the _____ glisten
And children listen
To hear _____ in the snow

"Away in a Manger"

Away in a manger
No _____ for a bed
The _____ Lord Jesus
Lay down His _____ head

"Silent Night, Holy Night"

Silent night, holy night
All is _____, all is bright
Round yon Virgin Mother and _____
Holy infant so _____ and mild
Sleep in _____ peace

"Rudolph, the Red-Nosed Reindeer"

Then one _____ Christmas Eve
_____ came to say
"Rudolph, with your nose so bright
Won't you _____ my sleigh tonight?"

"Frosty the Snowman"

With a _____ pipe and
a _____ nose
And two eyes made out of _____

SANTA

Test your Saint Nicholas knowledge to complete the crossword.

ACROSS:

3. Goes around his belly full of jelly.
5. Goes in the stockings of the naughty list.
6. Santa's suit is made of this.
7. Full of presents, Santa carries it.
8. Santa rides in this.
10. The top of your house.
11. Describes people who are getting presents.

DOWN:

1. Santa has a long white one.
2. _____ and cookies.
4. Made in Santa's workshop.
5. Santa comes down it.
7. Big sock hung up over the fireplace.
9. Santa checks this twice.

Stuck? See solution on page 122

12 DAYS OF CHRISTMAS

Find the words hidden in the letters below. It's easier than putting a partridge in a pear tree!

DANCING   GOLDEN   MILKING   TREE
DRUMMERS   RINGS   PARTRIDGE   PIPING
GEESE   LEAPING   PEAR   TURTLEDOVES

```
J  A  L  L  E  A  P  I  N  G  S  C  R  X  U
D  H  P  Q  D  Z  W  V  H  X  D  Y  Z  P  T
A  L  M  G  R  W  O  G  I  Z  L  Q  J  A  D
N  K  R  G  U  J  X  Q  T  M  E  W  K  R  F
C  F  C  O  M  F  U  O  U  W  J  F  X  T  L
I  P  N  L  M  U  X  Z  R  X  S  E  W  R  G
N  M  K  D  E  I  T  D  T  I  G  H  G  I  P
G  I  R  E  R  M  I  G  L  P  P  R  V  D  E
T  L  J  N  S  E  L  Q  E  T  I  E  Z  G  A
I  K  V  R  W  N  Y  U  D  E  R  P  R  E  R
B  I  H  I  Q  V  I  G  O  N  S  E  I  V  L
L  N  L  N  Z  Q  O  J  V  L  A  E  E  N  W
D  G  G  G  S  K  E  A  E  Z  S  X  O  P  G
V  B  T  S  T  K  S  Y  S  S  Q  O  A  F  X  N
S  Q  S  Z  C  S  Q  F  W  M  S  C  X  K  A
```

Stuck? See solution on page 122

CHRISTMAS EVE

You gotta be *kitten* me! Can you find all the items hidden in this Christmas chaos? **CLUES: 9 ELVES • 10 CANDY CANES • 9 SNOWFLAKES • 10 GINGERBREAD MEN**

Stuck? See solution on page 123

TOY STORY

Hot Wheels

Toy cars are always a good holiday present. Who doesn't love watching little cars speed along tracks, race down ramps, crash into each other, or even do loop-the-loops? But none of that fun would have been possible without Hot Wheels. Before Hot Wheels, die-cast cars—that's cars made out of metal to look like real cars—rolled slowly and were mostly made for looking at or pushing around with your hands. Yawn.

Hot Wheels broke the mould when they designed cars with thick, hard plastic wheels that rolled super fast. And instead of making the toy cars look exactly like cars on the street, Hot Wheels made custom cars in crazy colours with cool modifications. Now kids around the world play with Hot Wheels, and there are more Hot Wheels cars than there are life-size ones! Ten million Hot Wheels are made every week, and over 6 billion have been made since they started.

Even adults get in on the Hot Wheels action: some grown-ups are serious collectors of Hot Wheels, with the average collector owning more than a thousand cars. The most expensive Hot Wheels car was a special version of a Volkswagen minibus with surfboards in the back. It sold for over $70,000! A good find for a collector would be one of the original "Sweet 16" cars that Mattel first introduced. These cars

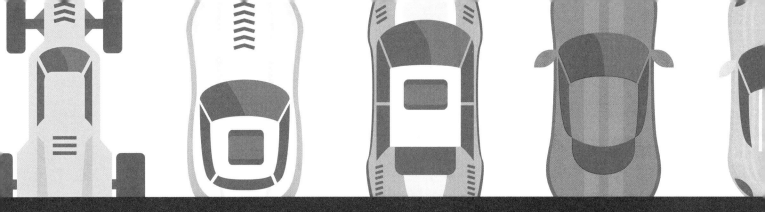

were inspired by muscle cars in California and included models such as Corvettes, Mustangs, Firebirds, and Pythons.

It's not just the cars that people of all ages love to play with. Hot Wheels tracks come in all shapes and sizes, and they can be connected in any way you can imagine. In Australia, someone must have gotten very tired of being stuck inside during the Covid-19 lockdown—they broke the world record for the longest Hot Wheels track! It was over 720 metres long, and the cars running on the track kept moving for 5 minutes without any power!

DID YOU KNOW?

Hot Wheels and Barbie are part of the same family—they were invented by a husband and wife, and they are made by the same company.

TRIVIA

✓X✓X✓X✓X✓X✓X✓X✓X

1. What was the first Hot Wheels car to be made?
(A) Red Mustang
(B) Blue Camaro
(C) Green Ferrari

2. What colour is a Hot Wheels track?
(A) Neon orange
(B) Cherry red
(C) Sky blue

3. The design team for the first Hot Wheels cars included
(A) A mechanic and an artist
(B) An architect and a race car driver
(C) A car designer and a rocket scientist

Answers: 1. (B); 2. (A) ; 3. (C)

HOLIDAY CRAFTS
TOILET PAPER ROLL TREES

Toilet paper is one of the most-used items in any household. You can turn the endless supply of empty rolls into cheery Christmas trees.

What You Need
Empty toilet paper roll(s)
Pencil
Small scissors
Green crayon, marker, or paint
Decorations: Sequins, dots, or buttons
White glue or glue stick

ANDY

AUNT LIZ

Tip: Turn toilet paper trees into place cards for the table by adding people's names.

What to Do

1. Use the pencil to draw a dot about 2.5 centimetres (1 inch) from the bottom edge of a toilet paper roll.

2. Draw a line all the way around the roll that starts and ends at the dot. Try to keep the entire line 2.5 centimetres (1 inch) from the edge of the roll. All of the cardboard below this line will form the base of your tree.

3. To mark the tree trunk, draw a square that is roughly 2 centimetres (0.75 inches) on each side. The bottom side of the square should line up with the top of the tree base.

4. Time to mark the triangle that will form the main part of the tree. Place your pencil on the top side of your tree trunk, in the middle. Lightly draw a straight vertical line up to the top edge of the roll. Draw a dot at the top of the line.

5. From one of the top corners of the tree trunk, draw a horizontal line that extends about 2.5 centimetres (1 inch).

6. Draw a diagonal line that connects the end of the horizontal line with the dot at the edge of the roll.

7. Repeat steps #4 and #5 on the other side of the tree trunk.

8. Now that you have marked your entire tree, cut away any cardboard that isn't part of the base, trunk, or main part of the tree.

9. Colour or paint the main part of the tree green.

10. Glue decorations to the tree.

Tip: Slip an LED light into the base of the tree to make it glow.

SNOW FAMILY LIKE OURS!

Find all eight differences between these happy snow families.

Stuck? See solution on page 123

WORDS FOR SNOW

Snow by any other name is still just as cold. Can you find these words for snow hidden in the letters below?

AZU   HIMA   IQHWA   LUMI

BORRA   HIMPAAT   IRIDIDI   NEIGE

CHIONI   INYEVE   KAVI

```
R  J  U  Z  J  X  V  D  H  F  B  Z  M  H  D
S  M  C  H  I  O  N  I  J  V  S  N  M  L  T
L  I  N  D  V  B  N  R  G  C  S  X  N  G  K
J  Z  B  R  U  D  T  C  X  F  W  L  B  F  I
B  B  L  R  Z  L  Z  U  L  M  G  V  E  T  Q
A  O  T  H  W  P  F  I  R  I  D  I  D  I  H
Z  O  R  R  S  W  X  T  X  Q  J  R  X  S  W
U  V  G  R  D  B  H  K  Z  D  U  A  S  K  A
G  G  I  G  A  Q  X  I  S  I  S  W  S  F  N
S  F  P  U  I  V  U  I  M  X  H  X  S  J  E
A  Z  E  W  H  J  G  N  K  P  J  N  C  N  V
B  M  O  F  M  P  S  Y  A  L  A  W  V  A  A
A  E  X  B  M  S  A  E  V  U  N  A  P  K  R
N  E  I  G  E  D  N  V  I  M  D  Q  T  Z  M
H  Y  Y  Q  G  X  N  E  U  I  G  H  I  M  A
```

Stuck? See solution on page 123

WINTER HOLIDAYS AROUND THE WORLD

There are holiday words *ho-ho*-hidden in the letters below. See if you can find the words from the list all by your-*elf*!

BODHI
BOXING DAY
CHRISTMAS

HANUKKAH
KWANZAA
NEW YEARS EVE

ROHATSU
ZARTOSHT NO DISO

Z B D B D H M N W L T C W E O
A B O N E W Y E A R S E V E Z
R R B X O P W H V U L A D H L
T J O K I Y N M T S P P S W I
O A D H V N S L E T T Q Z C K
S O H W A U G Z D D O K T H W
H O I X P T B D F V Y R C R A
T B U Q Q E S X A B F O L I N
N Y C B W D G U R Y P F C S Z
O G S Q L V S F O G D G O T A
D O O H G A A Q L H J F A M A
I V N K R N O I F E G M G A N
S D G Z S T A L P J G G A S F
O H A N U K K A H J E Q Z R U
G M T A H X J C D P D I H B H

Stuck? See solution on page 123

MERRY MASH-UP

How to Play

Before you read the story, fill out the requested list of words. Then, use these words to fill the blank spaces in the story. Want to supercharge the fun? Play with a friend! Ask them to give you each type of word on the list. Write their answers in the blank spaces of the story—and laugh until your belly shakes like a bowlful of jelly!

The Words You'll Need

Adjective:_____

Type of food:_____

Type of food:_____

Liquid:_____

Plural noun:_____

Adjective:_____

Verb:_____

Verb:_____

Adverb:_____

Verb:_____

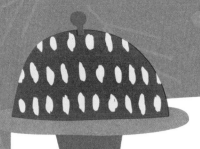

STUFF THAT BIRD!

Here's how you make Grandma's _____ (adjective) **turkey**

stuffing. First, you need to chop some _____ (type of food)**.**

The secret is adding a pinch of _____ (type of food) **and a**

drop of _____ (liquid)**. I also find** _____ (plural noun)

add a(n) _____ (adjective) **quality.** _____ (verb)

all of the ingredients together, then _____ (verb)

the stuffing into the bird as _____ (adverb) **as you can.**

Don't forget to _____ (verb) **Grandma for the recipe!**

CHRISTMAS BY THE NUMBERS

How do you eat a candy cane? The National Confectioners Association says roughly 60% of Americans start at the straight end, about 30% start at the curved end, and the rest break the candy cane into pieces.

WRAPPING PRESENTS

Guess the tools of the trade to wrap up this crossword puzzle.

ACROSS:

2. Easier than wrapping paper, has handles to carry it by.
4. Can be any colour, used to colour pictures.
6. Pictures that you can stick onto things.
8. Another word for "present."
10. Usually cardboard.
11. Usually black or blue, use it to write in the card.
12. Makes ornaments sparkle.

DOWN:

1. Made from trees, you write on it.
3. Can be white or purple, goes on sticky and dries clear.
5. Shiny, flat string for tying up presents.
7. Two blades attached together for snipping.
9. Sticky, to hold closed a lid or stick on wrapping paper, sometimes it's called "Scotch _____."
13. Where you write "To" and "From" on a present (there's also one on the back of your shirt).

Stuck? See solution on page 123

PRESENT

Can you find your way
through the maze
present-ed below?
Gift it your best shot!

Stuck? See solution on page 123

HOLIDAY CRAFTS
ELVES

You can create a whole workshop of elves with little more than scrap paper! Mix and match colours and designs to make each elf unique.

What You Need

Card stock or stiff paper in any colour or design

Scrap paper in any colour or design

Markers, coloured pencils, or crayons

Scissors

White glue or glue stick

What to Do

1. Draw face shapes and body shapes on the card stock or stiff paper. You can use our templates (see page 127) or create your own. If you are creating your own, be sure to add an extra 2.5 centimetres (1 inch) to the bottom of each elf body. You'll need this to make the stand.

3. Cut out the face and body shapes.

4. Draw features on the faces with markers, coloured pencils, or crayons.

5. Snip decorations for the bodies out of tiny scraps of paper. Make buttons! Hats! Arms!

5. Glue each face to a body.

6. Wait at least five minutes for the glue to dry.

7. Place each elf facedown on a flat surface. Fold the bottom 2.5 centimetres (1 inch) of the body to form the stand.

STOCKINGS

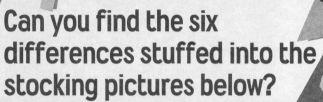
Can you find the six differences stuffed into the stocking pictures below?

Stuck? See solution on page 124

FUN IN THE SNOW

Can you find all the words hidden in the letters below? *Icy* them all.

BLIZZARD **CRYSTALS** **ICE** **SNOWBALL**
CHILL **FORT** **ICICLE** **SNOWFLAKE**
COCOA **FROST** **SNOW ANGEL** **SNOWMAN**

```
V F G B S N F H Z F Y D L Z W
Z Y Y X N X R H Q B A C C X L
O M B S O F O B Q A B V R Z I
S I Z T W L S H X K Y R Y X C
S N R D M X T J K P M A S C I
N F O X A L C Q C O R D T W C
O C P W N C F G X M F L A B L
W E S O F S H C O C O A L L E
B X V M B L F I C O S C S I K
A O C A J X A O L I N Z Z Z X
L O O J K K D K R L U C D Z D
L N I J C L J D E T L X J A T
F T C K S N O W A N G E L R K
M P E U W J K I F R F L Z D N
B Q O K M O X I E P K L J N K
```

Stuck? See solution on page 124

HOW CHRISTMAS BEGAN

Long before the arrival of Christmas, people in ancient times loved to throw a winter party. Many of these marked the winter solstice: the shortest day and longest night of the year. In the northern hemisphere, the winter solstice is around the third week of December. Afterwards, the days start getting longer and warmer—a great reason to celebrate!

Ancient peoples paid tribute to gods and goddesses during their solstice celebrations. For example, the Romans held a festival called Saturnalia in honour of Saturn, the god of sowing seeds. During Saturnalia, people held feasts and gave each other gifts.

The Birth of Jesus

Christmas is a Christian holiday that celebrates the birth of Jesus of Nazareth, also known as Jesus Christ. Jesus was a spiritual leader whose life story is told in the Bible and other Christian writings. One thing the Bible doesn't mention is Jesus's birthdate. In fact, it wasn't until the 4th century that leaders of the Christian church decided to observe Jesus's birthday on December 25. They may have chosen this date to fit with winter solstice celebrations.

The Secular Side of Christmas

In the 19th century, Christmas became more secular—that is, less religious. The holiday began to focus more on family, community, and togetherness. A lot of Canada's secular traditions arrived from England around this time, including carolling and exchanging Christmas cards.

CHRISTMAS DINNER

Can you s-*pie* all the items hidden in this festive meal?

CLUES: 8 CHRISTMAS CRACKERS • 8 CUPCAKES • 13 MICE • 9 CANDY CANES
• 6 HOLLY

Stuck? See solution on page 124

Nerf

Have you ever dreamed of an epic Nerf battle? Foam darts flying every direction, blaster designs, and a whole warehouse of space to play in? This dream is a reality at the Nerf testing facility. Members of the Nerf team try out prototypes and then work to improve them. The team tests the blasters in fake bedrooms, basements, offices, and more, all inside a big warehouse.

The first Nerf blaster shot foam balls when you pumped the handle. Later, Nerf introduced blasters that fired foam darts like the ones they make today. The first foam dart shooter was called the Sharpshooter. These blasters only shot one dart at a time. Today, Nerf makes blasters that hold and shoot lots of darts. The electric versions can shoot them much faster than pumping the handle of a Sharpshooter!

Nerf darts are made out of a unique foam called polyurethane that is very light and spongy. This means you won't be hurt even if darts hit you at fast speeds. Over 400 million

darts are made every year. That's over 4 billion darts since Nerf started making them! Nerf is named after the material its darts are made of. The same foam was used as padding in off-road racing. The racers called it NERF, which stands for non-expanding recreational foam.

DID YOU KNOW?

Nerf started with a ball. They called it the "world's first official indoor ball," and the ads encouraged kids to throw it inside! That's probably a bad idea no matter how soft and spongy the ball is.

TRIVIA

✓X✓X✓X✓X✓X✓X✓X✓X

1. The most powerful Nerf blasters can shoot darts up to what speed?
(A) Up to 20 kilometres per hour
(B) Up to 50 kilometres per hour
(C) Up to 80 kilometres per hour

2. How long does it take the fastest Nerf blaster to shoot 144 darts?
(A) 10 seconds
(B) 30 seconds
(C) 60 seconds

3. How many years passed between the Nerf ball and the Nerf blaster?
(A) 5 years
(B) 20 years
(C) 50 years

Answers: 1. (C) ; 2. (B) ; 3. (B)

MERRY MASH-UP

How to Play

Before you read the story, fill out the requested list of words. Then, use these words to fill the blank spaces in the story. Want to supercharge the fun? Play with a friend! Ask them to give you each type of word on the list. Write their answers in the blank spaces of the story—and laugh until your belly shakes like a bowlful of jelly!

The Words You'll Need

Verb ending in -ing:_____

Adjective:_____

Adjective:_____

Plural noun:_____

Verb ending in -ing:_____

Plural noun:_____

Plural noun:_____

Verb:_____

Verb ending in -ing:_____

BELLS ON WHAT?

_____ (verb ending in -ing) **through the snow**

In a(n) _____ (adjective), _____ (adjective) **sleigh**

O'er the _____ (plural noun) **we go**

_____ (verb ending in -ing) **all the way**

Bells on _____ (plural noun) **ring**

Making _____ (plural noun) **bright**

What fun it is to _____ (verb) **and sing**

A _____ (verb ending in -ing) **song tonight, oh!**

RUDOLPH'S ROOTS

Rudolph isn't just the only red-nosed reindeer—
he's probably the only male reindeer in Santa's
crew! That's because male reindeer drop their
antlers in early December, regrowing them in
February. Females, on the other hand, keep their
antlers during the Christmas season.

ACROSS:

3. Explosive snack, sometimes strung on a string for decorating.
6. Strings of these glow.
8. Fir or pine, has needles.
11. Big red fabric in fancy loops.
12. Wrapped around presents.

DOWN:

1. Has five points and glitters gold.
2. You eat straw and blue ones of these in summer.
4. Melt as they burn.
5. You often put before "cone."
7. Has wings and a halo.
9. On your foot, also finishes the word mistle_____.
10. Choo choo!

Stuck? See solution on page 124

Guess all the *tree*-mendous decorations to complete the crossword puzzle.

CHRISTMAS DECORATIONS

HOW TO DRAW SANTA

1. Draw a triangular shape with a rounded top and a curved bottom—like a thimble. Add two dots for eyes and a small circle or oval for a nose.

2. Add two banana-like shapes under the nose to make a moustache. Connect the top of the moustache to the sides of the face with two diagonal lines, then add two almond-shaped eyebrows above the eyes. Add a tiny half-circle under the moustache for a mouth.

3. Now, draw a curly or wavy line around the bottom of the face for a beard. Add a rectangle with slightly curved sides to the top of the head. Align the bottom of the rectangle with the eyebrows.

4. Draw a semi-circle on the left side of the body to make an arm. Draw two short horizontal lines on the right side for another arm. Add two squares to the middle of the body to create a belt buckle. Draw lines connecting the belt buckle to the edges of the body. Add a rectangular cuff to the end of the right arm. Draw a hat on top of the head.

5. Draw a pompom at the top of the hat. This could be a circle or more flower-shaped. Add mittened hands to the arms and boots to the legs.

6. Add a cuff to the end of the left arm. Draw a big circle to the right of the body to create a toy sack. Add a line from the hat down to the mitten on the left hand. Add a short line from the beard to the mitten in the left hand.

7. Colour in your drawing and say hello to Santa!

OTHER WINTER HOLIDAYS

Christmas isn't the only holiday game in town. Canada is a diverse country made up of many different cultures with their own traditions. Here are three other major celebrations that may be taking place in your community.

Hanukkah

Hanukkah is also known as the Festival of Lights. It's a Jewish holiday that lasts eight days and nights and takes place between late November and late December. Each night during Hanukkah, families perform a candle-lighting ritual using a special candlestick with nine branches, called a menorah. They may also exchange presents, sing hymns, play a game of dreidel, and eat traditional foods, such as latkes, brisket, and kugel.

Kwanzaa

The word "kwanzaa" was inspired by a Swahili phrase that means "first fruits." This celebration of African culture takes place every year between December 26 and January 1. Families and communities come together each day to light a candle and share meals, stories, history, music, and dance. Kwanzaa was created in 1966 by Maulana Karenga, a professor, author, and activist.

Sunlight Celebrations

Indigenous peoples throughout the northern hemisphere have been celebrating the winter solstice for centuries. It's a time for gratitude, rituals, listening to Elders, and preparing for the months ahead. In Canada's far north, the weeks after the solstice are a sacred period of hope, renewal, and joy. That's because many communities see little to no light for weeks to months in the wintertime. Local festivals are timed to celebrate first slivers of morning sunlight, which usually peek over the horizon in January.

HANUKKAH

Bet you Hanu-*can't* find all the celebratory words hidden in the letters below.

APPLESAUCE CALENDAR CHEESE LIGHTS
BLESSINGS CANDLES DREIDEL SUFGANIYAH
BUNUELOS CELEBRATION FESTIVAL SUNDOWN

```
T  O  D  M  V  S  D  A  D  Z  R  A  L  F  W
C  E  L  E  B  R  A  T  I  O  N  A  B  E  L
Q  V  Y  U  G  A  P  P  L  E  S  A  U  C  E
M  G  D  Y  R  V  R  T  Y  N  Q  Q  L  K  H
C  A  N  D  L  E  S  G  I  S  O  A  L  C  I
L  Z  Y  J  J  S  B  M  W  N  U  Q  I  H  S
S  U  F  G  A  N  I  Y  A  H  N  B  G  E  U
W  U  X  X  W  O  F  W  L  R  A  H  E  N  N
L  Z  W  G  B  U  N  U  E  L  O  S  T  S  D
D  R  E  I  D  E  L  N  U  S  X  T  S  E  O
V  X  W  U  E  U  N  Z  X  U  T  U  M  L  W
E  K  P  C  N  B  L  V  L  U  S  I  H  F  N
P  E  B  D  C  O  I  I  T  U  F  R  V  E  Q
T  D  B  L  E  S  S  I  N  G  S  R  O  A  F
V  J  C  A  L  E  N  D  A  R  Y  Z  A  C  L
```

Stuck? See solution on page 124

HOLIDAY CRAFTS
CLOTHESPIN PUPPETS
AND BIRDS

A clothespin is a decoration and hanger all in one!

What You Need

Clothespin

Markers

Optional: Coloured paper, scissors, glue

What to Do

Puppets: Draw a face on the side of a clothespin with markers. The metal hinge can be a nose and the round opening can be its mouth.

Tip: Pinch the clothespin so the mouth opens and closes while your puppet talks or sings a song.

Birds: You can use one of the templates at the back of this book (see page 128) to make birds out of coloured paper. (See "Using a Template" below.) Once you've got your birds, glue each bird to a clothespin and let dry for at least five minutes. Don't forget to add wings!

Using a Template

1. Lay a thin sheet of paper over a template.
2. Trace the shape onto the paper with a pencil.
3. Cut the shape out of the paper.

3. Place the paper shape over a piece of coloured paper.
4. Trace around the edges of the paper shape with a pencil.
5. Cut the shape out of the coloured paper, following the pencil outline.

COTTON SWAB PUPPETS

Look very closely and what do we see? A tiny cotton swab puppet looking back at you and me!

What You Need

Cotton swabs
Tweezers, sewing pin, or safety pin
Markers
Optional: Coloured paper, scissors, glue

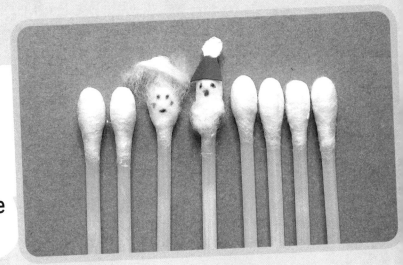

What to Do

1. Use tweezers, a sewing pin, or a safety pin to tease out some of the cotton to form hair or a beard. (Be careful with pins—the ends are very sharp!)
2. Add features to the face by making teeny dots with markers.
3. To add a hat or another accessory, snip a tiny shape out of coloured paper and glue it to the cotton or stick.

WHAT IS YOUR REINDEER NAME?

Have you ever wondered what your name would be if you were a fluffy, flying reindeer pulling Santa's sleigh?

Find out below by finding the first letter of your first name and combining that reindeer name with the name that goes with your favourite colour. Have two favourite colours? See what happens when you combine two last names!

A Appleton
B Bobtail
C Cha-cha
D Dearen
E Ebeneezer
F Fireball
G Greensleeves
H Hay-ley
I Ike
J Jolt
K Kris
L Lichen
M Mambo

N North
O Olive
P Polar
Q Quicksilver
R Rudy
S Skipper
T Tart
U Unicycle
V Venus
W Wallop
X X-mas
Y Yule
Z Zip

RED Rednose
ORANGE Hoofington
YELLOW Fitzrudolph
WHITE Snickerdoodle
BLUE Oatski
PURPLE Von Antler
PINK Carrotberg
GREY Rooftopper
WHITE Snowflake
BLACK Dasherstein
BROWN El Jingle
RAINBOW Caribou
GOLD Blitzbop
GREEN MacReindeer

THE REAL REINDEER

The following list has 30 reindeer names—but only nine belong to Santa's reindeer. Circle the names you think are the real deal. Turn the page upside down to check your answers.

Blizzard

Chestnut

Cupid

Jingle

Donal

Vixen

Randolf

Ginger

Comet

Dashel

Crystal

Sparkle

Blitzen

Aunt Ler

Dancer

Glitter

Venus

Dasher

Snowflake

Twinkle

Blixon

Prancer

Powder

Rudolph

Jangle

Dazzle

Donner

Flicker

Fluffy

Glisten

Answers: Dasher, Dancer, Prancer, Vixen, Comet, Cupid, Donner, Blitzen, Rudolph

MERRY MASH-UP

How to Play

Before you read the story, fill out the requested list of words. Then, use these words to fill the blank spaces in the story. Want to supercharge the fun? Play with a friend! Ask them to give you each type of word on the list. Write their answers in the blank spaces of the story—and laugh until your belly shakes like a bowlful of jelly!

The Words You'll Need

Noun:_____

Animal:_____

Noun:_____

Body part:_____

Body part:_____

Noun:_____

Plural noun:_____

Friend's name:_____

Liquid:_____

CHRISTMAS COLD

Christmas colds are the worst! I've been feeling under

the _____ (noun) **all week. As sick as a(n)**

_____ (animal)**, I tell you. It's hard to get into the Christmas**

_____ (noun) **when your** _____ (body part)

is as red as Rudolph's _____ (body part)**. At least I get to flop**

on my _____ (noun) **and watch my favourite**

_____ (plural noun)**. Maybe** _____ (friend's name)

will bring me their special _____ (liquid) **soup.**

HOLIDAY CRAFTS
TART TIN ORNAMENTS

Shiny dots make bright spots anywhere!

What You Need
Small tinfoil tart tins, either new or well-washed
Paper punch or scissors
Hangers: Pieces of string, ribbon, or dental floss, or partially unbent paper clips

What to Do
1. Press down the edges of a tart tin to form a flat circle.
2. Use the paper punch or scissors to pierce a hole close to one edge of the circle.
3. Run a hanger through the hole.
4. Tie or twist the ends of the hanger together.

Emboss:
To create raised markings on a surface.

FESTIVE FOIL SEALS

Don't throw away those foil seals from yogurt tubs and other food products! You can transform them into silvery holiday ornaments with fabulous textures.

What You Need

Foil seals from coffee tins, yogurt tubs, or other food products, washed

Paper punch or scissors

Hangers: Pieces of string, ribbon, or dental floss, or partially unbent paper clips

Optional: Dull pencil with a rounded tip for embossing

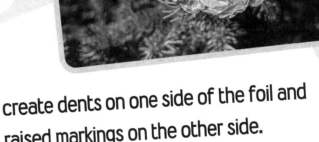

What to Do

To create a crinkly texture:

1. Gently crumple a seal into a loose ball.
2. Smooth flat again.

To emboss a seal:

1. Smooth out a food seal on a flat surface.
2. Using the rounded tip of a dull (not sharp!) pencil, gently press on the foil to draw shapes and designs. The pencil will create dents on one side of the foil and raised markings on the other side.

To hang a seal:

1. Use the paper punch or scissors to pierce a hole close to one edge of the seal.
2. Run a hanger through the hole.
3. Tie or twist the ends of the hanger together.

WRITE A LETTER TO SANTA

Santa loves receiving letters from around the world. Letters help him learn more about the kids he visits on Christmas Eve and to choose the perfect gifts for them. Here's a step-by-step guide to writing a great letter to Santa.

Getting Ready

Take some time to read these instructions and think about your letter before you begin.

Pick your paper and envelope. They could be plain, coloured, or even have a design. Your choice!

Choose something to write with, such as a pencil or coloured pencil.

Write your address in the top left corner of the envelope.

Write Santa's address in the middle of the envelope. If you're sending the letter through Canada Post, use this address:

Santa Claus
North Pole
HOH OHO
Canada

No need for a stamp! Letters to Santa can be mailed without stamps in Canada.

Finally, write your own address in the top right corner of your letter.

Writing Your Letter

Santa is an old-fashioned guy, so you might want to start your letter in the traditional way:

Dear Santa,

Tell Santa your name and age so he knows right away who is writing to him.

You could tell him other things about yourself. For example, the activities that you like to do or fun things that happened to you over the past year. Santa keeps an eye on every kid, but he loves learning more about you.

Now you can ask politely for the gifts you want this year. It's a good idea to ask for no more than three. This will help Santa understand what's most important to you.

If there's space on your paper, you could add a drawing of yourself, your family, or the gifts you want.

Don't forget to say thank you and wish Santa a safe trip.

Add a sign-off, such as "Sincerely" or "Best wishes," then sign your name.

Carefully fold your letter, place it in the envelope, and seal it.

Put your letter in the mail before December 7 to ensure it reaches the North Pole in time.

TOY STORE

Search the picture for the hidden items.
I know *choo-choo* can do it!

CLUES: 9 ROBOTS • 10 PRESENTS • 12 CARS • 12 BEARS •
5 DOLLS • 3 ROCKETS • 7 DINOSAURS

Stuck? See solution on page 125

Silly Putty & Slime

One is stretchy and bouncy, while the other is gooey and gloopy, but Silly Putty and slime have a lot in common. Both toys use forms of the element Boron to make stretchy polymers, similar to rubber or plastic. Silly Putty is made from boric acid and silicone oil. Slime can have many different recipes, but common ones include guar gum or white glue plus borax. These combinations make something rubbery that is not quite solid and not quite liquid. You can play with and mould the putty or slime like clay, but if you leave them on a hard surface, they will slowly spread out like a puddle. Just don't leave Silly Putty or slime on something soft like clothes or furniture. They will ooze into the holes in the fabric and become almost impossible to remove.

Silly Putty has even more strange properties. It bounces when dropped gently but shatters when thrown hard. It stretches when pulled slowly but snaps if given a sharp tug. In 1989, a university student wondered what would happen if they dropped Silly Putty from the roof of a building. They tried it with a 100-pound ball of putty. It bounced first, then broke when it hit the ground again!

While slime is just fun to play with, Silly Putty can also be used to solve important problems. Astronauts on the Apollo mission used Silly Putty to stick their tools down without gravity. The putty is sticky enough to clean dirt, fur, or ink off of things. Doctors use it to help patients strengthen their hands after injuries. A zoo in the United States even used Silly Putty to make moulds of gorilla paws!

DID YOU KNOW?

Silly Putty is sold in egg-shaped containers because it was first marketed near Easter.

Slime was first sold as Gak, a bright green goo inside a garbage can-shaped container.

TRIVIA

✓X✓X✓X✓X✓X✓X✓X✓X

1. The earliest record of a slimy substance is from the 1700s. What was the Swedish scientist looking at under a microscope?
(A) Snot
(B) Moss
(C) Slugs

2. Silly Putty was invented by accident during World War II. What material were scientists trying to replace when they discovered it?
(A) Rubber
(B) Elastic
(C) Glue

3. How many eggs of Silly Putty have been sold since the beginning?
(A) Over 3 million
(B) About 125 million
(C) More than 300 million

Answers: 1. (B); 2. (A) ; 3. (C)

POPSICLE STICK AND SPOON PUPPETS

Grab a handful of wooden popsicle sticks or spoons to make portable pocket puppets that can perform anywhere!

What You Need

Popsicle sticks, stir sticks, tongue depressors, or disposable bamboo spoons

Clothes and accessories: Paper scraps, ribbon, beads, buttons, small pieces of yarn, or other small items

Markers

Scissors

White glue

Optional: Cotton swabs and tape

Tip: If you want to attach cotton swab arms, skinny pieces of tape will stick better than glue.

What to Do

1. Decide which characters you want to make. Parents or siblings? Monsters, reindeer, fairies, bugs?
2. Draw silly faces on the wood with markers.
3. Add clothes and accessories, such as hats and scarves, with glue.

MERRY MASH-UP

How to Play

Before you read the story, fill out the requested list of words. Then, use these words to fill the blank spaces in the story. Want to supercharge the fun? Play with a friend! Ask them to give you each type of word on the list. Write their answers in the blank spaces of the story—and laugh until your belly shakes like a bowlful of jelly!

The Words You'll Need

Your last name:_____

Adjective:_____

Family member's name:_____

Type of food:_____

Beverage:_____

Family member's name:_____

Room in the house:_____

Verb ending in -ing:_____

Animal:_____

Family member's name:_____

A LETTER FROM SANTA

Dear _____ (your last name) **Family,**

I am writing to apologize for Christmas Eve. All was

_____ (adjective) **when I arrived. Or so I thought! I was**

startled by _____ (family member's name) **coming out of the**

bathroom. This caused me to drop the _____ (type of food)

you left for me. And the _____ (beverage) **spilled all over**

the floor. As I was cleaning it up, _____ (family member's name)

suddenly emerged from the _____ (room in house)**!**

_____ (verb ending in -ing)**, but still asleep!**

Well, I finished my work as quick as a(n) _____ (animal)**.**

On my out, I tripped over _____ (family member's name)**,**

asleep on the floor.

WINTER WEAR

Gear up to guess the answers to this cold-weather crossword.
You won't be worse for wear when you finish!

ACROSS:

2. Thermal underwear, _____ Johns.
4. To use for stomping footprints in the snow.
7. Puffy overalls to keep your legs warm.
8. Long or short, sometimes knitted.
9. Be sure to put a woolly pair of these on your feet.
12. Winter hat, very Canadian.
13. Lighter than other winter wear for your top half.

DOWN:

1. To keep your hands warm, one space for all the fingers and another for the thumb.
3. To keep your hands warm, individual finger spaces
5. Special coat with a fur-lined hood.
6. These are fuzzy and keep your ears warm.
10. Heavier winter outerwear, can have a hood.
11. This will be cold if you don't put on a scarf.

Stuck? See solution on page 124

YULE

Look closely and *yule* find the words hidden in the letters below.

CELEBRATE   LONGEST   SHORT   WINTER
COLD   NIGHT   SPRING   YULE
DAYLIGHT   RETURNING   WAIT

```
D  R  B  U  H  Y  P  N  S  H  O  R  T  Z  W
C  U  E  L  D  W  S  P  R  I  N  G  E  R  A
O  G  B  O  A  A  L  I  J  X  I  I  O  C  M
L  G  Q  N  W  H  W  Y  D  Z  H  E  K  C  S
D  Y  S  G  M  A  U  N  G  P  S  H  F  E  I
Q  U  C  E  R  W  I  R  Q  Q  C  T  T  L  L
B  L  G  S  R  E  I  T  F  K  X  J  I  E  L
R  E  A  T  W  M  T  N  I  M  T  P  A  B  S
N  P  D  N  R  W  I  U  S  X  Z  P  R  T
H  B  Y  I  K  V  L  Z  R  E  T  L  X  A  R
W  L  V  G  J  V  N  O  G  N  R  Y  R  T  R
R  Y  J  H  O  C  N  I  U  G  I  R  O  E  N
A  Y  Q  T  K  V  K  U  V  K  V  N  G  H  G
U  F  L  F  A  A  J  C  B  H  R  V  G  X  A
A  V  C  D  A  Y  L  I  G  H  T  C  W  R  A
```

Stuck? See solution on page 125

HOT CHOCOLATE HOT TUB

Stuck? See solution on page 125

Spot the six sweet and salty differences between these marshmallow snowmen.

CHRISTMAS EVE CUSTOMS

In many countries, Christmas Eve's traditions are as important as Christmas Day's. They may even be *more* important! Let's follow Santa's sleigh tracks around the world to learn about different Christmas Eve customs.

Central America

Several countries in Central America and South America set off fireworks on Christmas Eve. These include Mexico, Guatemala, El Salvador, Colombia, and Peru. First, people attend a late-night church service, then they enjoy the fireworks display around midnight.

Venezuela

In Caracas, the capital of Venezuela, people roller skate to Christmas Eve church services. Many streets are closed to traffic to help keep everyone safe.

Iceland

Icelanders love to give books as presents, then curl up to read them on Christmas Eve. This ritual is known as Jólabókaflóðið, or "Yule Book Flood."

Ireland

Irish families place a single red candle in the window on Christmas Eve. The tradition may have started as an invitation to priests to visit the household. Another theory is that the candle relates to the Bible story of Mary and Joseph struggling to find an inn on Christmas Eve. The candle is a symbol that Mary and Joseph are welcome.

France

In parts of France, families prepare 13 desserts to follow their Christmas Eve dinner. 13! These remain on the table for the next three days.

Poland

Polish families eat a huge Christmas Eve feast called Wigilia. It's traditional to not eat all day and to only start the Wigilia after the first star appears in the sky.

HOW TO DRAW A SNOWPERSON

1. Draw a circle. This will be your snowperson's head.

2. Draw the sides and bottom of a rectangle below the circle to make part of a scarf. Give the bottom line of the rectangle a slight curve.

3. Now add a larger circle under the scarf. Draw an even larger circle under the second one.

4. Face time! A narrow triangle with a curved bottom gives you a carroty nose. Add two dots for eyes and a row of dots for the mouth.

5. An oval shape on top of the head will become the brim of a hat. Another oval, hovering above it, will become the top of the hat.

6. Connect the top and brim with two slightly curved lines. Between these two lines, draw a horizontal line to form the base of the hat.

7. Add a straight line to each side of the body to create stick arms. Add two more small lines to the end of each stick for twig-like fingers. Add two rectangles of different sizes to the scarf to finish it off.

8. Add stripes to the scarf and dots down the middle circle for buttons. Add a second horizonal line above the base of the hat to make a ribbon. If your snowperson is feeling fancy, finish off by adding a flower or another decoration to the hat.

9. Colour in your snowperson and watch it go—thumpety, thump-thump, over the hills of snow!

UNDER THE TREE

Toy with the following clues to find the answers to this playful crossword puzzle.

Stuck? See solution on page 125

ACROSS:

2. Cuddly stuffy named after a "grizzly" type of forest animal.
5. Toy that looks like a mini person.
6. Kids dream about finding this pet under the tree.
7. Build amazing things with these little plastic bricks.
8. Little warm clothes for your feet.
10. Comes with a present, but you have to read it first!
12. Gift that you can read.
13. Warm, fuzzy piece of clothing for your arms and body.

DOWN:

1. Sweet treats, can be chewy or hard.
3. Bounce this or play catch with it.
4. Toy with four wheels, you can carry and dump sand with it.
9. Wax that can be all different colours, for drawing.
11. For riding in the springtime, has two wheels.

TANGLED LIGHTS

What a mess! Help the elf find the right cord to plug in the Christmas tree.

Stuck? See solution on page 125

SANTA'S REINDEER

Deer-ect your attention to the following clues to complete this en-deer-ing crossword.

DOWN:

1. What birds do in the sky.
3. "All of" the other reindeer, heard wrong (it's a name or a snack).
4. Reindeer will do this to salt or other minerals they need.
5. Reindeer would like to eat this, also a snowman's nose.
6. These grow out of every adult reindeer's head.
7. They wouldn't let Rudolph join these.
9. Object in space made of ice and dust.

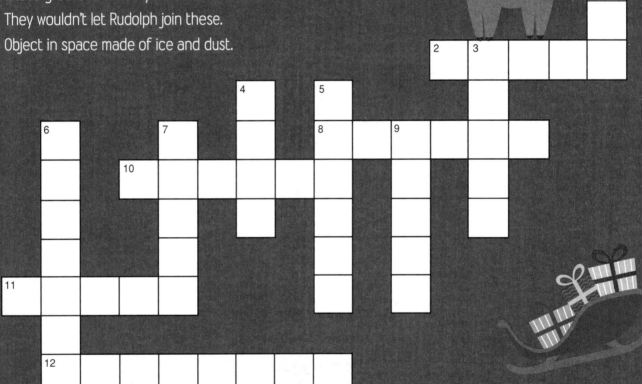

Stuck? See solution on page 126

ACROSS:

2. Misty, need Rudolph's red nose on this type of Christmas Eve.
8. Reindeer live here.
10. Someone who moves their body to music.
11. These make a jingling sound on the sleigh.
12. Reindeer are very good _____. They can go far in water.

HOW TO DRAW RUDOLPH

1. Draw two circles side by side. The left one should be a bit larger and lower. The right one should be smaller and higher.

2. Connect the circles with two curved lines. Add a little banana-shaped tail to the outside of the left circle.

3. Draw an ear near the top of the right circle and a snout on the right side of the circle. Try giving them slightly curved sides for a natural look.

4. Add a few details to the face, including eyes, a mouth, and a circle for that famous nose.

5. Now, we get to the trickiest part. Draw a back leg on the left circle. Start the leg about halfway up the circle. End it about halfway up the circle on the other side. Then draw a front leg on the right circle. The front leg should be bent at a right angle.

6. Add two more legs behind the first two.

7. Draw antlers on top of the reindeer's head. Antlers have multiple tines—the spiky bits. Add as many tines as you'd like!

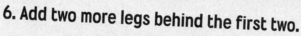

8. Nearly there! Draw tiny lines around the nose to show it's glowing. Add more tiny lines to the bottoms of the legs to create hooves.

9. Colour in your drawing. Don't forget to make Rudolph's nose bright red!

UNPACKING BOXING DAY

Raise your hand if you thought Boxing Day was for boxing up your gifts. Or breaking down gift boxes. Or lying around in your boxer shorts. Turns out, it's none of the above!

Boxing Day is celebrated on December 26 in the United Kingdom and many Commonwealth countries, including Canada, Australia, New Zealand, the Bahamas, South Africa, and Nigeria. It started in the 19th century as a day off for the servants of rich families. Some historians believe the name comes from the boxes of food and gifts given to these servants by their employers. Others say it comes from a holiday tradition of collecting money and other donations for the poor in boxes.

Mummering

In Newfoundland and Labrador, December 26 is a day for mummering, or mumming. The "mummers" disguise themselves in costumes and go to different homes in their community to perform plays, sing songs, or tell jokes. Guessing who is in the costumes is part of the fun. Once the masks are lifted, the mummers are offered food and drink.

In Ireland, December 26 is known as St. Stephen's Day or Wren Day. Irish mummers parade from house to house, carrying a pole or branch with a type of bird called a wren on top. In the old days, they demanded money from their hosts! This tradition dates back to at least the late 1600s.

Junkanoo

For more than 500 years, December 26 has marked the start of the Junkanoo carnival in the Bahamas. Its centerpiece is a joyous street parade filled with colourful costumes, music, and dancing. Community groups compete to be named the best entertainment in the parade.

NEW YEAR'S EVE

Don't drop the ball on finding these New Year's words hidden in the letters below.

CHANGE DANCING MIDNIGHT SPARKLERS
CLOCK FRIENDS PARTY TOAST
COUNTDOWN JANUARY SINGING TWELVE

```
K  S  C  K  M  G  C  E  U  F  Y  I  D  N  I
G  B  B  T  L  I  H  P  W  A  J  Q  A  S  I
O  A  I  Y  V  C  D  L  U  A  P  M  N  T  W
D  N  G  U  J  W  E  N  H  X  X  Y  C  W  S
L  R  F  O  N  A  U  L  I  V  X  D  I  E  U
C  C  R  W  B  N  N  P  W  G  E  L  N  L  E
K  C  I  C  O  X  V  U  Y  L  H  A  G  V  I
D  H  E  T  O  Z  H  A  A  E  E  T  C  E  W
B  A  N  O  K  U  S  P  A  R  K  L  E  R  S
C  N  D  A  G  U  N  Z  F  Z  Y  L  H  O  F
L  G  S  S  S  P  P  T  Z  A  S  L  Z  O  X
O  E  W  T  H  L  A  Z  D  D  T  D  P  S  B
C  N  P  J  A  R  G  R  D  O  U  Z  E  B  Y
K  M  U  F  I  V  I  D  T  V  W  S  P  O  Q
S  I  N  G  I  N  G  N  G  Y  M  N  I  A  G
```

Stuck? See solution on page 126

MERRY MASH-UP

How to Play

Before you read the story, fill out the requested list of words. Then, use these words to fill the blank spaces in the story. Want to supercharge the fun? Play with a friend! Ask them to give you each type of word on the list. Write their answers in the blank spaces of the story—and laugh until your belly shakes like a bowlful of jelly!

The Words You'll Need

Noun:_____

Noun:_____

Plural noun:_____

Verb:_____

Adverb:_____

Adverb:_____

Adjective:_____

Place:_____

Noun:_____

NEW YEAR'S RESOLUTIONS

New year, new me! Time to turn over a new _____ (noun).

I swear on my _____ (noun), I will treat my parents

like _____ (plural noun). I will _____ (verb) my room

every week and do my chores _____ (adverb). Not only

that, I'll eat _____ (adverb) and be _____ (adjective)

around my teachers. Most importantly, I'll spend more time at the

_____ (place) to be the best _____ (noun) I can be.

WINTER PLACES

Which of these is not a real place?

A. Snowflake, Manitoba

B. Sled Lake, Alberta

C. Tinsel Town, Nova Scotia

D. Reindeer Station, Northwest Territories

E. Holly, Ontario

Answer: C.

Lego

Although they hurt to step on, nothing beats LEGO bricks when it comes to toys for building. From castles to space-ships, LEGO has sets with instructions to build almost anything in the world, real or imagined. Even better, almost every kid has a big bin of loose LEGO parts somewhere that they can build without instructions to come up with truly unique creations. These bricks can be clicked together in endless ways because they are designed with tubes that interlock, or fit together, tightly and snugly. The LEGO brick in its current form has been around for over 60 years, and its design hasn't changed: you can take a new brick from the store and fit it together perfectly with the LEGO that your parents played with as kids. You can even fit the small LEGO bricks with the larger DUPLO blocks that your younger siblings might play with.

LEGO has been used to make all kinds of things, from replicas of famous monuments to an actual house! The life-size LEGO house used over 3 million bricks, and it had a shower and toilet that worked, as well as a very hard plastic bed. Speaking of huge LEGO projects, the record for the tallest LEGO tower is over 28 metres, and it was made from 465,000 bricks. Those are some big creations!

LEGO master builder is a real job, not just something in the LEGO movies. LEGOLANDs in ten locations around the world hire people to build their models and attractions. But LEGOLAND isn't the only place you can see LEGO creations on display. The Art of Brick is an art exhibit made entirely of LEGO that travels from place to place for kids and grown-ups to explore. It seems like for LEGO the recipe for toy success is making something so simple that, like it says on the box, anyone ages 4—99 can enjoy it.

DID YOU KNOW?

The name "LEGO" was made up by combining the first two letters from each of the two Danish words for "play well": Leg Godt.

There are enough LEGO bricks for every person on earth to have around 80.

TRIVIA
✓X✓X✓X✓X✓X✓X✓X✓X

1. If you laid all the LEGO bricks sold in one year end to end, how many times would they wrap around the whole world?

(A) 1

(B) 3

(C) 5

2. How long does it take a LEGO brick to break down in the environment (biodegrade)?

(A) 100 years

(B) 1000 years

(C) It will never happen

3. The LEGO moulding process is extremely accurate. Out of a million bricks, how many do not meet the quality control standards?

(A) 18

(B) 56

(C) 150

Answers: 1. (C); 2. (C); 3. (A).

WHO AM I?

Let's see if you can guess the name of this mystery character from just a few hints. Turn the page upside down to see the answer.

1. Like Santa, I'm known for being jolly.
2. My eyes are black.
3. I'm known for wearing a top hat.
4. I have a pipe, but would never light it.
5. I'm not a fan of hot weather.
6. Don't worry if I leave. I'll come back again one day.

Your answer:_____

Answer: Frosty the Snowman

WHAT AM I?

Let's see if you can guess this mystery item from just a few hints. Turn the page upside down to see the answer.

1. I'm as sweet as can be.
2. Almost 1.8 billion of me are made each year.
3. I'm usually two colours, sometimes more.
4. My shape may have been inspired by shepherds.
5. I'm most popular during the second week of December.
6. I like to hang around during the holidays.

Your answer:_____

Answer: A candy cane

WHERE AM I?

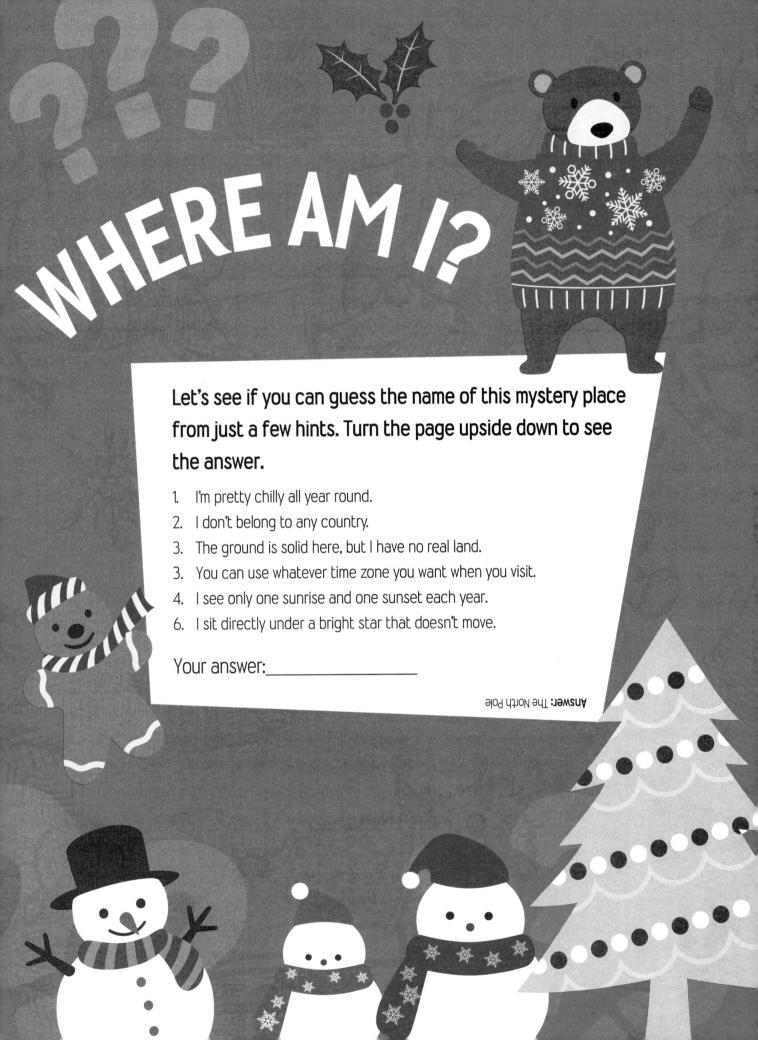

Let's see if you can guess the name of this mystery place from just a few hints. Turn the page upside down to see the answer.

1. I'm pretty chilly all year round.
2. I don't belong to any country.
3. The ground is solid here, but I have no real land.
3. You can use whatever time zone you want when you visit.
4. I see only one sunrise and one sunset each year.
6. I sit directly under a bright star that doesn't move.

Your answer:_____

Answer: The North Pole

HOLIDAY ORNAMENTS

These ornaments will have you seeing *bauble*. Find 12 differences between these two pictures.

Stuck? See solution on page 126

HOT CHOCOLATE

Hot chocolate is yummy on its own—and even yummier when you add extra flavours! First, make the basic recipe and adjust it to your taste. It's a good idea to start with the smaller amounts of sugar and cocoa, adding more if you want. Then, choose an extra flavour to add to each mug.

MAKES 4 SERVINGS

Ingredients

1/4—1/2 cup	Cocoa powder
1/4—1/2 cup	Sugar
4 cups	Milk
1 teaspoon	Vanilla extract
Pinch of Salt	

SAFETY FIRST!

- Don't cook or bake without alerting a grown-up.
- Wash your hands before you handle food.
- If you have long hair, tie it back.
- Make sure the kitchen equipment and surfaces are clean.
- Confirm you aren't allergic to any of the ingredients.

Instructions

1. Gather all of the ingredients.
2. Add the cocoa, sugar, salt, and a 1/2 cup of milk to a saucepan. Whisk to combine.
3. (A grown-up may need to do the next steps or supervise while you do it.) Place over medium-low heat. Continue whisking until everything is fully dissolved.
4. Whisk in the rest of the milk.
5. Turn up the heat to medium. Whisk frequently until hot enough to serve. (You want to see steam, but no bubbles.)
6. Remove from the heat. Stir in the vanilla.

Extra flavours

Marshmallows—big or small, and as many as you can fit! • Dollop of whipped cream • Drop of peppermint oil • Crushed candy cane (or use one as a stir stick) • Dash of ground cinnamon • Squirt of bottled caramel sauce (or a spoonful from a jar) • Sprinkle of orange zest • Spoonful of peanut butter • Feeling spicy? Add a teeny pinch of cayenne pepper for a little kick.

HOLIDAY COOKIES

You're a smart enough cookie to find these *crumb*-y words hidden in the letters below.

BRUNKAGER   GINGERSNAP   SHORTBREAD
CHOCOLATE   KRUMKAKE   SNICKERDOODLE
EGGNOG   LINZER   SUGAR
GINGERBREAD   PEPPERMINT

S	O	M	Q	C	Q	O	L	Z	Y	K	R	U	C	K
C	N	R	S	H	O	R	T	B	R	E	A	D	R	V
H	F	I	B	V	U	Y	V	K	H	O	K	F	O	U
O	Q	I	C	G	I	N	G	E	R	B	R	E	A	D
C	D	E	B	K	O	W	J	X	A	I	U	S	W	P
O	A	G	U	R	E	Z	W	O	Q	W	M	U	S	E
L	Z	G	Y	J	U	R	X	T	A	D	K	G	I	P
A	T	N	N	S	G	N	D	U	L	H	A	A	L	P
T	K	O	D	U	U	K	K	O	J	Z	K	R	I	E
E	E	G	H	K	J	H	T	A	O	N	E	T	N	R
O	A	Z	L	D	U	M	V	B	G	D	L	E	Z	M
J	S	K	C	H	C	G	K	Y	Y	E	L	F	E	I
C	G	I	N	G	E	R	S	N	A	P	R	E	R	N
N	C	H	F	Z	G	U	V	L	C	O	U	M	S	T
G	S	S	N	Z	W	Y	D	Y	R	L	R	O	Q	M

Stuck? See solution on page 126

TREE-REX AND TREE-CERATOPS COOKIES

The peanut M&M'S on top of these cookies crack during baking—and look like hatching dinosaur eggs! Use only the green and red M&M'S to make your dino eggs festive. You can also swap them for plain M&M'S, chocolate chips, or chocolate squares (one square per cookie).

MAKES ABOUT 18 COOKIES

Ingredients

1 Egg	
1 tablespoon	Vanilla extract
1 cup	Dark brown sugar
1/4 cup	White sugar
1 teaspoon	Orange zest
1/2 teaspoon	Sea salt or Kosher salt, plus extra for sprinkling
1 cup	Chunky peanut butter
1/2 cup	Shredded coconut, unsweetened
1/2 cup	Peanut M&M'S—green and red eggs

SAFETY FIRST!
- Don't cook or bake without alerting a grown-up.
- Wash your hands before you handle food.
- If you have long hair, tie it back.
- Make sure the kitchen equipment and surfaces are clean.
- Confirm you aren't allergic to any of the ingredients.

Instructions

1. Preheat the oven to 350°F.
2. Line two baking pans, or two cookie sheets, with parchment paper. (If you only have one, you can bake the cookies in two batches. Let the pan cool between batches.)
3. Gather all of the ingredients.
4. Wash the orange. Ask a grownup to help you zest it. Set aside.
5. Crack the egg into a large bowl. Lightly beat it with a fork or whisk until the white and yolk are combined.
6. Add the vanilla, brown sugar, white sugar, orange zest, and salt. Stir together with a spatula or wooden spoon.
7. Add the peanut butter and mix thoroughly.
8. Stir in the coconut.
9. Scoop generous tablespoons of dough and form them into balls. Place on the baking pan, about 4 centimetres (1.5 inches) apart. Press the dough lightly with your fingers to make the top more flat.
10. Press a few peanut M&M'S into the surface of each cookie. Sprinkle the cookies with a small amount of salt.
11. **A grown-up may need to do the next steps or supervise while you do it.** Put the baking pans in the oven and bake for 10—12 minutes.
12. Remove the baking pans using oven mitts and rest them on top of the stove or another safe surface. Leave the cookies on the pans to firm up for at least five minutes. Carefully transfer the cookies to a wire rack to cool completely. They will continue firming up as they cool.

SOLUTIONS

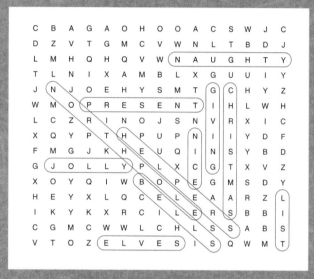

Santa's Workshop

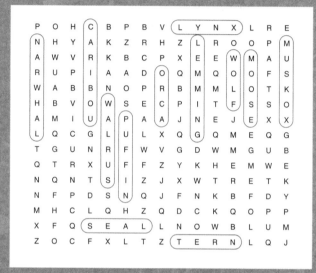

North Pole Animals

The North Pole

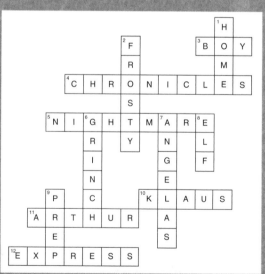

Holiday Movies

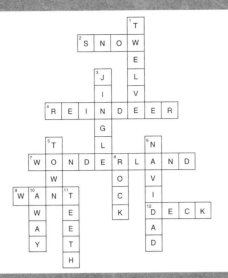

Christmas Songs

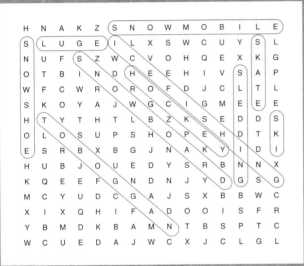

Winter Sports

Christmas Tree

Gingerbread House

The Nutcracker

Snow Difference

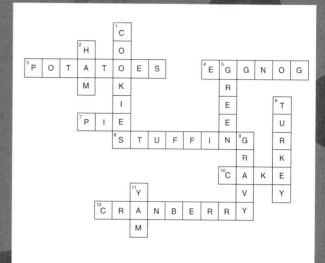

Holiday Dinner

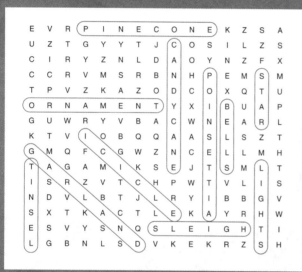

Tree Decorations

Snowman

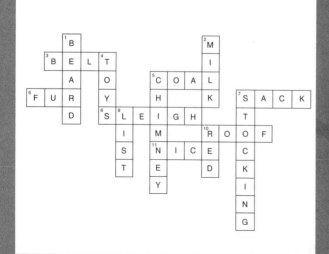

Santa

12 Days of Christmas

Christmas Eve

Snow Family Like Ours

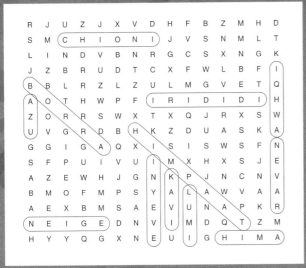

Words for Snow

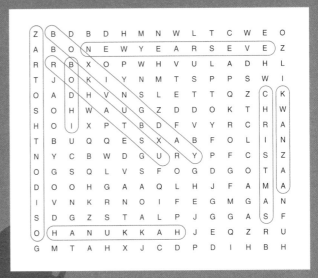

Winter Holidays Around the World

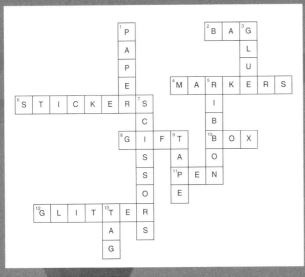

Wrapping Presents

Present

123

Stockings

Fun in the Snow

```
V F G B S N F H Z F Y D L Z W
Z Y Y X N X R H Q B A C C X X L
O M B S S O F B Q A D A R Z X I
S I Z T W L S H X K Y R Y S C C
S N R D M X I T K P M A T C I L
N O F O X A N L C Q C O R D A E
O C P W N C F G X M F L A L
W E S O F S H C O C O A S W B
B X V M B L F I C O S C B L
A O C A J X A O L I N Z Z I I
L O O J K K D K R L U C D Z Z
L N I J C L J D E T L X J A D
F T C K S N O W A N G E L R T
M P E U W J K I F R F L Z N
B Q O K M O X I E P K L J N K
```

Christmas Dinner

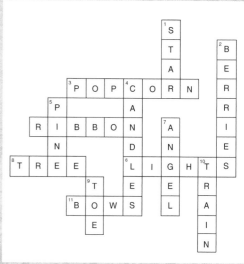

Christmas Decorations

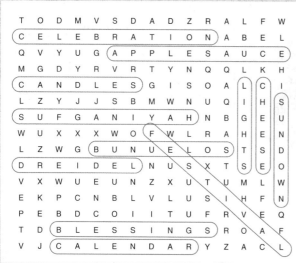

```
T O D M V S D A D Z R A L F W
C E L E B R A T I O N A B E L
Q V Y U G A P P L E S A U C E H
M G D Y R V R T Y N Q Q L K H
C A N D L E S G I S O A L C I
L Z Y J J S B M W N U Q I H I
S U F G A N I Y A H N B G E U
W U X X X W O F W L R A H S N
L Z W G B U N U E L O S T E D
D R E I D E L N U S X T L D O
V X W U E U N Z X U T U M L W
E K P C N B L V L U S I H F N
P E B D C O I I T U F R V E Q
T D B L E S S I N G S R O A F
V J C A L E N D A R Y Z A C L
```

Hanukkah

Winter Wear

Toy Store

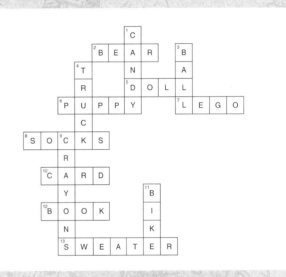

Under the Tree

```
D  R  B  U  H  Y  P  N (S  H  O  R  T) Z  W
C  U  E  L  D  W (S  P  R  I  N  G  E) R  A
O  G  B  O  A  A  L  I  J  X  I  I  O  C  M
D  Y  S  N  W  H  W  Y  D  Z  H  E  K  C  S
Q  U  C  G  M  A  U  N  G  P  S  H  F  E  I
B  L  G  E  R  W  I  R  Q  Q  C  T  T  L  L
R  E  A  S  R  E  I  T  F  K  X  J  I  E  S
N  P  D  T  W  M  T  N  I  M  T  P  A  B  P
H  B  Y  N  R  W  I  U  T  S  X  Z  P  R  R
W  L  V  I  K  V  L  Z  R  E  T  L  X  A  I
R  Y  J  G  J  V  N  O  G  N  R  Y  R  T  I
A  Y  Q  H  O  C  N  I  U  G  I  R  O  E  G
U  F  L  T  K  V  K  U  V  K  V  N  G  X  A
A  V  C (D  A  Y  L  I  G  H  T) C  W  R  A
```

Yule

Hot Chocolate Hot Tub

Tangled Wires

125

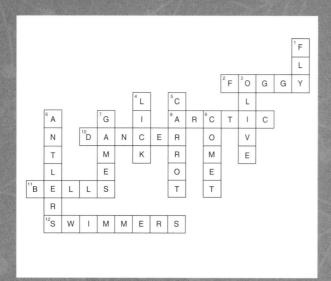

Santa's Reindeer

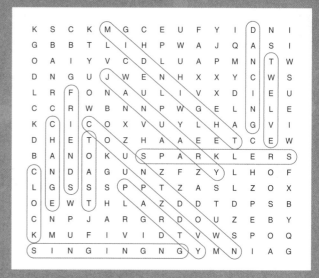

New Year's Eve

Holiday Ornaments

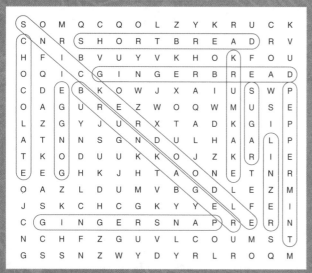

Holiday Cookies

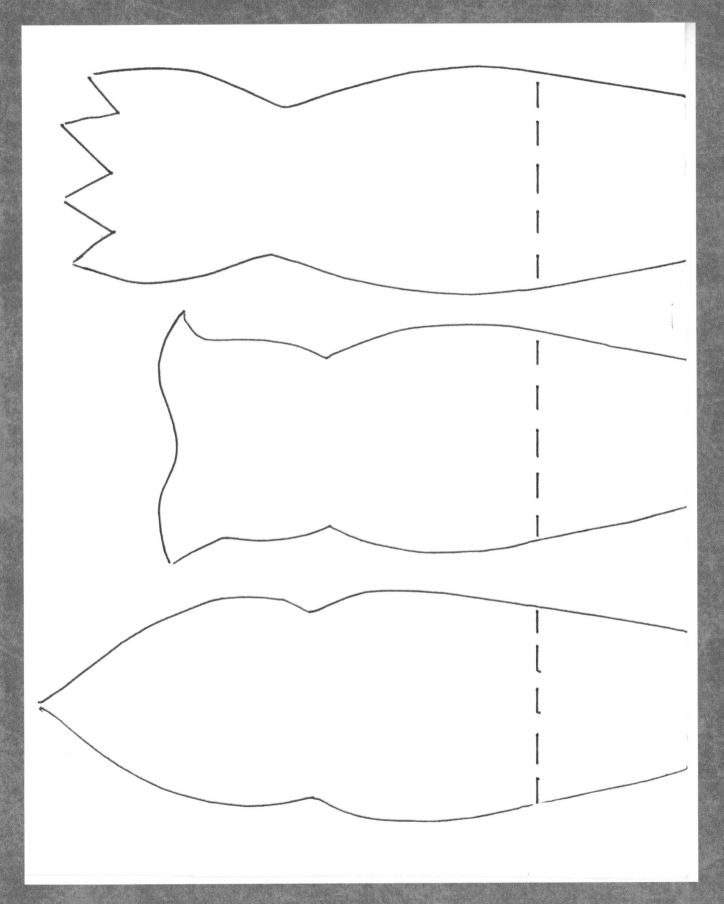